BEYOND THE COUCH

BEYOND THE COUCH

by Eileen Walkenstein, M.D.

Crown Publishers, Inc., New York

Inquiries should be addressed to Crown Publishers, Inc., 419 Park Avenue South, New York, N.Y. 10016.
Library of Congress Catalog Card Number: 72–84301
ISBN: 0–517–500434
Printed in the United States of America
Published simultaneously in Canada by General Publishing Company Limited

To my parents, Ethel and Ben, who gave me the fiber to stand up;
to my brothers, Sid, Bob, and Marv, who tested that fiber in our
     struggles to grow;
to my children, Danny, Tara, Seth, and Merissa, to whom I hope
     I have given some of that fiber;
and to the flourishing fiber of humanness in all earth's children.

CONTENTS

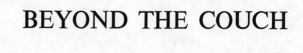

BEYOND THE COUCH

1

TENSION · VERSUS TRANQUILIZERS

Listen, we're living in an age in America when everyone wants to suck a tit and not enough mamas are offering. So what's happened is the production of a whole bunch of ersatz mamas in the persons of medical doctors, psychiatrists, and other pill pushers; and ersatz tits in the form of tranquilizers, sleeping pills, pot, alcohol, and dope. Whereas real milk from real mamas benefits our growth . . . our growing up . . . the ersatz stuff benefits the pharmaceutical companies and the crime syndicate, and in the case of the booze tit, the government gets the benefit from high taxes. So with all these profits from puppetry, the little guy is growing down, not up, in America. Aah, well, I'll get back to him later. I'll just say for now that he gets no benefit at all—on the contrary!

Why am I carrying on about all this ersatz feeding? I really do get stirred up about it. It's like this—there's something in the contemporary drug scene, legitimate (so-called) and illegal, that carries with it a profound contempt for bodies in their natural, real, organic, human state . . . a disrespect for the living animal tissues in the person. This alienation from one's own body, which drugs "help" readily to accomplish, is the start of the generalized alienation between people. Like, how can I not be alienated from you if I have already estranged myself from my vital innards, my animal anxieties, and my human concerns by using one form of drug or another? The very philosophy of our medical-drug age is antithetical to human growth and development. The doctor who dispenses tranquilizers–sleeping pills–sedatives as readily as he would sugar pills is preventing himself and his patients from facing a common human dilemma. I consider drug dispensing for allaying anxieties to be essentially antihumanistic!

When I was in my internship in 1951, there was a doctor in the obstetric-gynecology department, a giant hulk of a man, much respected in the medical community for his technical skills. When he learned of my interest in psychiatry, he said: "I can't for the life of me understand how anyone in his right mind would willingly go into that field. As for myself, I can't stand to have some of these women come in and complain about all their woes. I'd go crazy if I hadn't found a way out for myself." He had devised a method of slowly counting each tooth in his mouth with his tongue while his patient was communicating her distress, and, by concentrating carefully on the counting, he didn't have to listen to her, thus allaying his own tensions. I wonder what kind of feeling those women had who reached out to him for help while he was withdrawing into his tooth count. And was he not already a little crazy, to trade his and his patients' humanity in for a dental mathematical computer? One good shot like "you're boring me with all your complainings and I'm getting tense" would have cleared up the entire deal and made two human beings more real to each other. But no one takes the risk, and today's doctor has a more sure-fire method of squelching the personal contact: he gives the patient a tranquilizer and/or takes one himself.

Another facet of this dehumanizing process is the happiness kick we're on. Imagine—I get patients who tell me their motivation for coming into treatment is to be happy. Damn! I'm all for mother's milk and gratification of basic needs and all that, but I thought the contented-cow-happy-ever-after-fable died with Santa Claus. I'll be damned if I'm in the cow production business—I'll leave that to the mother cows . . . and I guess there are enough contented cattle chewing their cud in America's pastures so that we don't need psychiatrists to turn out any more of them. No!—what we need are live, intact human beings. My motto—well, one of them—is "suffer, then you know you're alive and we can go on from there." Pain is part of joy and let's never forget it. Isn't it clear that happiness is not a goal of life, but a happy by-product? Why isn't this clear to everyone? What's the matter, America, are you suffering from national myopia? I can't think of an analogy startling enough to make this point clearer—it's so bright it dazzles me—who ever heard of "looking for happiness"? And even more astonishing is the notion that a pill can find it for you!

When I go to see a sunset over the ocean I go to see a sunset over the ocean—my thrill, awe, wonderment, joy, happiness at being part of this scene is precisely the by-product of the scene. I don't go to the ocean *looking* for these sensations or I'd never encounter them. Happiness isn't something I *find*—it's something that happens—a happening if you will. And sometimes in that scene of the setting sun I find pain, sorrow, poignancy, a sense of bereavement, a pang of nostalgia—I don't go looking for these things either—they happen as much as the joy happens—a by-product of the equation of me and where I am—inner me contacting outer me and getting together with a resultant set of emotions.

Thirty-five-year-old Susan, who had been in traditional psychiatric treatment for several years, made an appointment to see me. She was in severe tension, close to panic, ready to explode out of her head, and yet ridiculously saying she came to see me because she wanted to be happy. I told her, right off, in that first session that she didn't "need" to be happy, and that what she needed to do immediately was to confront her panic and we'd better get to it right away. She was sitting on the edge of the seat, her hands

13

clutching the arms of the chair, her eyes wide open with pupils dilated in fear. She said she couldn't do that, that she was afraid of going crazy. "So what if you go crazy?" I asked.

S: Then I'd lose control altogether.

E: And if you lost control altogether?

S: I'd wind up in a booby hatch.

E: And if you wound up in a booby hatch? (She paused, smiled, showing visible signs of relaxation, and spoofed:)

S: Then I'd have nothing more to worry about. (Her laughter ensued, and she sat comfortably back in her chair as we laughed together.)

E: And what are you feeling right now, Sue?

S: I'm relaxed.

E: Good! Are you ready to work now?

S: Yes.

E: All right—what you've just said was that the worst thing that might happen to you is that you'll have nothing more to worry about. (She laughs again and we smile together.) Now, keeping this in mind, are you willing to confront your panic and work it through?

S: Yes.

E: Good! Now I'd like you to get back to that panic feeling you had before and allow yourself to experience it fully. (Pause—she closes her eyes and visibly begins to tighten and stiffen up, her face in a grimace as if pained.)

S: I'm frightened. (Her breath is held in, her face pale.)

E: What of?

S: I don't know.

E: Where do you feel it? (I almost always locate the bodily representation of the emotional state, bringing the body-psyche-emotions into an integral relationship for me and for the patient. She puts her palm alternately on her chest and midabdomen.)

S: Here . . . and here. (Her voice is coming out jerkily, her breathing very shallow.)

E: What's the worst thing that can happen to you right now?

14

S: I can lose control of myself.

E: What does that mean?

S: I would go wild.

E: And how do you picture yourself going wild?

S: I'd lose control of my body.

E: And if you lost control of your body?

S: I might fall off the chair.

E: All right—would you do just that—let your body go and fall off the chair. (She hesitates; I encourage her to let go and experience whatever there is to experience, and she begins to shake. I encourage her to just let herself fall off the chair . . . and then she does so . . . and she's lying on the floor in a heap, turns on her back, and begins to scream. As she screams I tell her to let herself experience what she's feeling—I'm down on the floor next to her. I remember my own conflict as to whether to hold her arm in "reassurance"—reassuring myself, maybe?—which might have been a type of subtle restraint on her fully experiencing, pulling her back from fully contacting her demoniac panic . . . and then I decided in one of those split-second type of decisions to just stay close to her but not touch her—not bring her away from the full and *necessary* experience of confronting her fear. Her screams are accompanied by convulsive movements and go on for several seconds (they feel like hours!).

As her screams subside, I remind her she can feel free to experience her panic and scream whenever she chooses to, knowing that she can also choose to stop—the experience is within her control. We are still on the floor together—she opens her eyes and smiles at me.

E: You did a good job, Sue—I know it was hard work.

S: Yes. (She sighs deeply and smiles.) On the way out of the office, she embraces me. She has moved through the panic and tension toward her strength and indeed looks quite happy.

She has faced her ordeal—and gone through the fire—and now feels at peace. She need never fear going through the fire again; she has now achieved a successful precedent for all such fiery confrontations. Despite having had recurrent panic reactions for the few years preceding that session, in the several months of therapy following that first session, she never again experienced such intense panic. The usual "supportive" type therapy would have had me accept her idiotic "happiness" goal, patting over her panic, and thus allowing it to grow underground.

Life is a matter of *discovery*—a great big question mark. A nineteen-year-old stiff, whispery university student came to see me because of severe, unrelenting headaches. She had been the usual route of family doctor, internist, allergist, and neurologist, and had been given all varieties of tests, X rays, medications . . . the headaches persisted and pursued her as avidly as she pursued the doctors. In our first session she insisted that everything in her life was "fine" except for the headaches. Her life was neatly packaged and she had no major questions. But I had plenty . . . and I confronted her with them: "How come you're so nice . . . you're so polite . . . how come things are so fine while your parents are against your boyfriend . . . how come it doesn't bother you more . . . how come nothing bothers you?" By the end of her next visit her headaches were gone, but things were not so "fine" anymore. She discovered that she was guilt-ridden, enraged at her invalid mother, furious at and fearful of her repressive, tyrannical father, and terribly inadequate as a woman. Before leaving our second session, this girl who had gotten mostly A's throughout her entire school career said: "Before, I knew all the answers; now I have only a question mark and I feel anxious." My response: "Good! You're alive! Now our work can really begin." (Incidentally, as soon as she began improving and feeling more secure about herself, her mother became ill, satisfying the seesaw arrangement of their relationship.)

There is only one neat, unquestioned place where everything is laid out for us. Of course, this is the final laying-out place . . . the final resting place . . . the ultimate peace . . . the coffin. You want to have all your questions answered, be totally at peace with no anxieties—perfection? . . . then get into your coffin now.

16

As for me, I would rather lie anxiously with a man alive than be laid peacefully in a coffin . . . and yet people go around life coffining themselves, being safe, secure.

"What do you get out of your marriage?" I asked a new patient who was having marital problems and trouble with her kids. "Security" was her unhesitating reply. She had no love, sparse and inadequate and unfulfilling sex, no communication or companionship, much hostility—all this and security too. "What do you do with your time?" I asked. "Play cards and bowl once a week." Geez, how much security does a person need to pursue these interests? That's about all this kind of security is ever worth—the equivalent of a game of cards and a bowling match. Can I look at the sky and feel my breathing, pulsing personness, my touch with the cosmos that's part of me whether I know it or not, in this security? Can I look into my loved one's eyes and feel my love reverberating back, in this security? No card game can feed my real needs. What price does that woman pay for security, exchanging her womanhood for a card game!

Look, it's not that I'm knocking card-playing . . . I'm wailing the human waste that clings to an ersatz security while life oozes away. Besides, I used to play cards myself when I was nine or ten and the boys would let me in the game . . . and my father even now plays pinochle with the men at the Friendship Corner when there's a game he can get into. (If he had made it in music, he'd be a famous mandolinist today. Instead, he got his fame as a paperhanger—the best in Philadelphia at a time when workers still took pride in their work. You don't find wallpaper seams so tight fitting anymore—seams, like people, are apart or slopped together.)

Getting back to security: I never saw security coming from externals like status (marital, financial, or educational) . . . these factors often help but are not critical. Hey, wait . . . I'm going off the deep end here and feel myself bullshitting me and you, so I'll just drop it right now and stick to what's bugging me. The thing that hung me up here was the question of the ghetto life and the numerous insecurities there—related to being a have-not

17

in a society of haves (in material things, of course; it's reversed when it comes to soul and gut things), a belong-not in a society of belongers, a white-not in a society of whites. Well, so I go off the deep end from time to time like anybody else. That's life— as soon as you make one encompassing, definitive descriptive statement about it—oops! up come the paradoxes, contradictions, contrarieties.

A twenty-two-year-old woman, Rhoda, tells me that her two-year-old marriage has been dreadful, accented by numerous attempts to separate from Mike, her twenty-four-year-old husband whose prime interest is business. She always returned to him because of "security." Mike likewise had told me he was afraid to leave Rhoda because he feels "insecure" without her.

In one session with Rhoda I created for her my picture of her marriage . . . I pressed my fingers hard against each other, my elbows resting on the arms of the chair making an inverted V. I asked her to mimic me and she responded instantaneously: "Yes, that's just like us—we lean on each other."

E: Now see what happens: When you remove one hand, the other falls down. (I demonstrate this and ask her to do likewise.) With both of you leaning on the other for security, it is impossible to stand upright on your own two feet without disturbing the equilibrium and someone's getting hurt. Well, that's the way it is. The only way to stand on your own two feet is to stop leaning and take a chance on hurting or getting hurt. (I demonstrate this by putting my hands upright, parallel to each other.) Now look what I can do—I can move close and touch while still standing upright (I bring my upright palms together, touching). As soon as I start to lean (pushing my fingers together and thereby separating my palms, again making an inverted V), we can no longer touch each other fully—we can only lean.

I asked Rhoda to do this and experience the touching and the leaning and somehow the whole play with our hands made sense to her for she left the session with a renewed resolve to take some steps toward independence. I was really glad she helped me discover this little arm and finger play. I could tuck it away for another time and it would subsequently always be mine to share with another patient who needed some contact with the destructive contactless elements in the pseudosecurity of leaning on another.

While we're on the subject of hand play . . . I saw a forty-eight-year-old obstetrician's wife, Bertha, who complained that her husband spent too much time with his medical practice and not enough time with her. "I tell him if he would only treat me half as well as he does any one of his patients I'd be happy. He has all the time in the world for them . . . when he's home he'll spend hours on the telephone listening to their complaints, but he never has time to listen to me." Her constant nagging only made him angry and more removed from her and increased her own tensions. She pushed, prodded, and yelled at him at every turn. He was a quiet-spoken man who swallowed his anger and threw himself more deeply into his work where he received much respect and admiration from his patients. When Bertha was not being angry with him, she would be worried about him, that he was overworked, and that he might die of a heart attack—these thoughts always made her feel tense and she suffered from headaches and shooting pains around her heart.

In one session, after Bertha had expressed concern about her overworked husband, I asked her to fantasize her severe pushing to the point where the poor guy had no recourse but to kill himself. Resisting me every step of the way, she finally gave in, faced his suicide, wept over his dead body, and at the end of the session she felt relaxed and calm and was resolved to stop pushing him. For one week they had an idyllic relationship "like the good old days," and I felt that maybe the gruesome suicide fantasy had perhaps turned the tide. But despite her concern over what she was doing to him, she resumed her nagging much to my dismay—I really believed in the magic of that suicide session that had gotten very fancifully gory indeed, with the gore dripping and spurting all over the bathroom where he had accomplished the deed in her fantasy.

19

So, in the next session, not only was she back in full swing with her nagging, but also meddling as vigorously as ever in the lives of her married son and daughter and driving herself buggy with worry in the process. She had grasped on to those three lives and refused to let go . . . and wondered at the same time why she had insomnia, headaches, and heart pains.

It suddenly occurred to me to show her what it felt like to literally hang on to another person, so I asked her to reach out to my outstretched hands, lock her fingers in mine, and pull against my pull. We stayed deadlocked that way for a while, straining our muscles against each other until my biceps and finger joints ached —I told her to note her tension as she stayed holding on, refusing to let go—how she imprisoned not only me but herself as well, and this was what she was doing to her husband and married children. My arms felt that they were breaking off when finally, at long last and in the nick of time, she said it hurt too much, that she had to let go. "Good!" I said, "just let go and see how it feels." She let go and I let go simultaneously. My fingers were pale and numb by this time. "See how good it feels to just let go," I said as I tossed my hands lightly in the air, reducing the tension in my muscles and moving my hands freely in an outward direction. She mimicked my hand motion, smiled, and said in a relaxed manner: "Oh, that feels good." She tossed her hands out several times, open-palmed, and then smiled broadly, almost beaming. She asked me to remind her to do "that thing with my hands" every time she started to clutch. Incidentally, in all the years of Bertha's adulthood she had never done anything alone outside of her home . . . her intense pushing, meddling, clutching was her attempt to avoid facing her loneliness. Had she simply faced her loneliness and made peace with it years ago, through her tensions and fears she would have contacted her strength and might have saved years of clutching at the evanescent security found in other people's innards.

Several weeks after that session, when I had almost forgotten our little hand play, she reminded me that this was one of the best things she had gotten out of treatment so far, and whenever she felt herself starting to push and nag she just made this light open-palmed gesture of throwing her hands in the air and would smile to herself and feel immediate relief. She later went on to develop a more independent stance, stopped her intense clutching at her husband and children, and entered into a more cooperative relationship with her husband.

Instead of facing up to basic situations like this, my big beef—and I'm fanatic on the subject—is how we evade and try to chemically make it easier for ourselves, even put ourselves to sleep, and how profit-making doctors, aided by bigger profit-making pharmaceutical companies, help us do it. The easiest way . . . the nearest way . . . is to raid the medicine chest: a pill is there to deaden our life's processes, disturb our natural hormonal flow, push us up when our body's reality is asking to let it stay down, put us to sleep when our body is restless and needs to move away from the cause of restlessness. We've gotten so far removed from our body, we no longer hear it. The only thing we hear is the pill's voice, not our own. And so begins the process of dealing death slowly and surely to our failing body.

You know, a pill is so much a part of a woman's wardrobe these days that she can even go into an exclusive department store or jewelry store and buy beautifully jeweled pillboxes to carry her hormones, aspirins, saccharine, barbiturates, tranquilizers, excitants, depressants, analgesics, ad nauseam. Yes, hide the disgusting horrible wasting of human vitality and feeling by bedecking the waste-giver—the death pill—with jewels and precious stones. And while I'm on the subject . . . besides the fatalities, the blood clots, and other abysmal side effects of the contraceptive pill, to say nothing of the depressions and increased tensions suffered by its users, the pill itself lulls a woman's wakefulness—that alive something inside every woman telling her when she's ripe to have a baby—the eternal woman's eternal inner voice—damn, we've gotten so far removed from our inner voices, from our primitive selves! Listen to this one: when I was in Mount Sinai Hospital, New York City,

21

nursing my first one-day-old baby, the young woman who shared my semiprivate room looked at me with repulsion: "Oh, how can you stand to do that? Why if I did a thing like *that* [and here her face screwed up into a dried prune, the juices in her swelling breasts dammed back and drying with synthetic hormones . . . and nature outraged], if I did a thing like that I'd feel like—like such an *animal!*"

Did you forget that we *are* animals—but alas, more similar to the domesticated pet variety who take on their masters' neuroses as children do their parents'—we are upright bipeds whose heads have replaced our guts.

Our technological age has produced the concept of the human animal as a machine, a computerized robot . . . or vice versa, namely the mechanized human animal has produced the age of technology as an extension of his own mechanization. Robots and all other machines, of course, should be perfect—perfectly performing, predictably reacting to what's fed into them . . . hence, feed them the "correct" data and you can get them to go to war and kill human beings, even defenseless ones, maybe especially defenseless ones. Perhaps this same mechanizing attitude forms the basis of the perfection craze we have in America. It's so extreme, this perfectionism, that we even cut off parts of the body that "may" tend later to cause trouble in a certain minute percentage of the population, like widespread circumcision, routine appendectomies during abdominal surgery, etc. . . . at one time it was routine tonsillectomies—who among us over thirty has tonsils left in his throat? Why stop with the foreskin . . . and the appendix?— might as well start excising the upper outer quadrant of all women's breasts to prevent the cancer that may arise at this site!

How idiotic that we fall for this perfection craziness! The bombardment of our population with tranquilizers-sedatives-soporifics (with their natural offspring of marihuana, LSD, mescaline, and the like), together with the use of brain killers like electric shock and lobotomy is part of this cutting craze—cutting out nature's signals of anxieties, problems, restlessness, tensions, sleep disturbances, boredom. These signals are yelling and screaming for *dealing with,* not *cutting out,* the underlying life message struggling for emergence. To be human in the world at this time *is* to be anxious. You really do have to be crazy altogether or nonhuman to encounter the world as it is, and as we are, without feeling some anxiety.

Tension and anxiety are necessary for therapy . . . and for life. As I've said, I see the dulling effects of tranquilizers as being contraindicated for therapy . . . and for life. What makes people sick is their withdrawal from conflict and tension, which only makes the conflict situation loom more threateningly; when they shut themselves off from their tensions, they shut themselves off from their life force. In therapy I welcome all openings to jump into the tension area with the patient . . . and things do get tense all right.

Jim was fearful that his fifty-year-old wife who was planning a short trip alone might indulge herself sexually. He felt hopeless to deal with his fantasies of her promiscuity, and the more he pushed these intolerable thoughts off the more threatened he was by them and the more futile his life seemed to become. He said: "I can really tear myself up into pieces when I think about it." Jumping in, I presented an exaggerated picture to him.

E: You picture her screwing a different guy every night.

J: Yeah.

E: Hanging from the chandeliers in the mornings.

J: (Laughs) Yeah.

E: A bunch of gigolos following her morning, noon, and nighttime too . . . through the night, six different guys an hour.

J: (Serious and solemn again) So I'm closing my mind off to that one, because if I don't close my mind off to that I would probably go file papers for a divorce.

We went on in the session to confront more vigorous images of his wife's sexual excesses. At one point I asked him: "Do you see her seducing your sons?" He thought a long while before answering, and I offered: "You haven't thought of that, huh?" He

23

responded, "No," and then with much laughter admitted: "She hasn't got that much sex drive!" The paradox of this response coupled with his fears of her sexual encounters was not immediately clear to him, but it was a significant first step in reducing the intensity of his fears and in seeing his rather cold, unsexual wife more realistically.

Getting back to pills, I'd like to remind you of the effects of a sleeping pill that almost flooded the American market—thalidomide. This was one of the most popular sleeping pills, sold over the counter in Germany from 1957 to 1961. Other countries also sold this drug, which caused over five thousand children to be born without arms and legs, with hands coming directly out of their shoulders and bearing resemblance to flippers of a seal (phocomelus).

Several United States pharmaceutical companies experimented with the drug, involving thousands of doctors and patients. In fact, a prominent United States company planned to market the drug. On November 29, 1960, this company's newssheet mentioned that 762 studies using the drug were planned. The salesmen were told to *push* the drug. A medical newspaper quoted the company's statement to their salesmen: "Appeal to the doctor's ego—we think he is important enough to be selected as one of the first to use X [their name for thalidomide] in that section of the country."

How do you like that for a sales pitch—appeal to the doctor's ego! Yes, ego, profits, keeping up with the Joneses, power, be the first, and never mind the inhuman consequences of your ambitious drives—never mind the tears and torment of those thousands of parents whose infants were being made into human seals with flippers. Get a good night's sleep, ladies and gentlemen—the drug that gives you tonight's tranquil sleep may be tomorrow's murdering monster; but that's tomorrow . . . in the meantime, sleep tight!

Yes, the ravages and the pillage of the Pill Age are truly upon us.

The drug salesman (detail man) doesn't miss a single detail of a selling trick in pushing the doctor into buying his company's product . . . *and he pushes!* . . . not the crass obvious way the men's clothing salesman on Philadelphia's South Street used to (probably still does) push—no, this is a sophisticated programmed pusher, programming the doctor with the latest modern computerized-guaranteed-to-sell methods with gifts as an added seducement. The robotized doctor programs his patients, the researcher uses the freely given drugs on guinea-pig patients in hospitals and writes his preconcluded "scientific reports" in medical journals (free advertising for the drug company) and gives his "scientific papers" at medical meetings (more free drug advertising) . . . when at the root of all this onslaught is a salesman just trying to make a buck to feed his family while the big macher (big shot) of the drug company can feed his private airplanes and yachts. Drugs, Medications for Profit! —I can't get over this fact—we are pushed drugs for profit, not for *health!* It's an unhealthy system—drugs for profit! Maybe it would help get some purity into drug research if the government took over the whole damn drug industry . . . and eliminated the individual company's need and greed. Maybe then we'd eliminate the dangerous drugs that cause our blindness, our deafness, our intestinal ulcerations, our deaths. Like there was this great anticholesterol agent, *MER/29,* that was avidly prescribed by doctors until it was forced off the market because the trouble with it was that, while it was great with cholesterol, it caused reversible baldness and irreversible visual defects (cataracts). Judging from the rate at which I receive mail from the FDA and the drug companies themselves warning of horrible side effects of drugs that they are removing from the market (after how many thousands have been harmed or killed?), I would guess that there isn't a family among you that hasn't at least one member suffering from some damage by some drug somewhere along the line.

As for elevated blood cholesterol and heart disease, some nutritionists ran a study which concluded that eliminating sugar from the diet altogether would help solve the problem. And maybe they're right. But medical doctors look on such simple, nonprofit preventive measures as faddist, while the food fads perpetrated by doctors themselves outweigh all others. What with the cholesterol scare . . . it's hard to find real whole milk, cow-nature's way, any more in

25

anybody's refrigerator. Instead, for their coffee, people use nondairy products that, like most ersatz things we eat and drink, contain poisonous products such as artificial flavorings, artificial colorings, and preservatives—many of which have been outlawed in other countries for their damage to health. Margarine, too, even pure corn oil margarine, has the artificial junk in it. And now even the airlines have joined the fad . . . so, you pour the poisonous noncream into the poisonous caffeine with the poisonous artificial sweetener—and, enjoy your flight in good health!

In November 1971 the FDA mailed a drug bulletin to doctors warning them against giving the hormone diethylstilbestrol to pregnant women because of a possible connection with producing cancer in the vagina of the offspring. And now, finally, all estrogens are required, "because of their possible danger," to contain a *warning* label as being contraindicated in pregnancy. There are example on example of the hazards and disasters of medical drug use. While drug research and some associated risk are necessary, I'm certain much of the hasty devastation would be eliminated by removing the underlying greed-profit motive.

Talking of governmental control of drugs and drug research, here's that contradiction that's inevitably on the other side of the complexity: namely, the stupidity of the United States government in maintaining a law that perhaps the majority of its citizens is breaking—I'm referring to the illegality of marihuana. The only thing this law seems to be accomplishing is to keep the police busy and to increase the ire and the number of dissenters—but we'll get to them later. Pot smoking is a symptom, similar in some ways to boozing . . . and laws against symptoms are as fruitless as chasing after hordes of flies with a fly swatter instead of removing the garbage in which they are breeding.

Furthermore, maybe what I feel is that what anyone puts into his own body (or wants to take out of it, as with abortions) is not a governmental or political matter at all but rather a private affair. I'm definitely concerned about the legal and illegal poisons people put into their bodies, and in my work with patients I fight it as much as possible, but I also feel it is their basic right to make this choice for themselves.

The crime syndicate doesn't hold a candle to the doctor syndicate when it comes to pushing drugs. But, just as the pill stands between our body and our feelings, so a chasm often stands between the word and the behavior—especially of professionals wheeling and dealing in the "legit" drug scene. Psychiatrists are masters at the use of the right words, while their actions bear abysmally little or no connection with their verbalizations. On the editorial page of the Official Newspaper of the American Psychiatric Association (Volume V, Number 15) is a piece entitled "On Pill Pushing." The editor is upset with Dr. W. Palmer Dearing, an admittedly "distinguished public health physician, always highly regarded in psychiatric circles," who had the nerve to criticize physicians and especially psychiatrists for pill pushing. Apparently Dr. Dearing had given "lurid" examples of the "potentially devastating end result of the widespread practice of prescribing and seeking tranquilizers and stimulants as antidotes to the pains, stresses, and monotonies of living" in an issue (August 1970) of Group Health and Welfare . . . (right on, dear Dr. Dearing!).

Right or wrong, psychiatrists who are members of "The Club" are supposed to keep their differences out of sight of, and present a united front to, the public. This totalitarianism is rationalized away by such concepts as "medical ethics" (one doctor is not supposed to say anything negative about another doctor, no matter what abuses he perpetrates . . . and certainly never to a patient!) and by such notions as: we don't want to cause anxiety or panic . . . the layman *(you!)* cannot handle the truth . . . we must keep things simple and unified. Thus, typically, the psychiatric editor attempts to vindicate psychiatrists against Dr. Dearing's charges, and he refers to a public statement made back in June 1945 by the American Psychiatric Association expressing concern for the widespread use of the recently developed tranquilizers. In 1955 three out of every ten compounds prescribed were tranquilizers (I wonder if it's tripled since then?) and the APA warned about the danger of the casual use of these drugs. The editor gets downright maudlin lauding psychiatrists who, among all doctors, "most often think twice before prescribing a pill." Let me tell you, there's no damn evidence for this! . . . Where is the unusual psychiatrist who lets his anxious patient out of his office without tranquilizing pills? Psychiatrists may be thinking twice, but it's surely not the patient's real needs that are being thought of . . . most probably it's the question of which tranquilizer should they use to settle his complainings and complaints. It's extremely rare for me to see a patient, either referred by another psychiatrist or who has been in treatment with one formerly, who is not taking tranquilizers—and often several different drugs at the same time. *There is no tranquilizer that can replace human interaction*—on the contrary, it diminishes and limits it.

The editor's last comment is a beautiful example of the word-deed schism: "We applaud and share Dr. Dearing's concern about the insidious growth of drug dependence in the United States. But we lament his singling psychiatrists out as a root cause and hope that he will perceive the lack of substance in his hasty generalizations." I have visions of this editor's burning the heretic Dr. Dearing at the stake unless he recants his heresy . . . fortunately it's the 1970s and not the 1600s.

I remember reading the June 1970 issue of a popular magazine and coming across a lengthy article with many photographs about a group of people in New York, including ministers, educators, mothers, ex-junkies, etc., who had started a war on dope and dope peddlers. The title in sharp letters sang out: "Blacks Declare War on Dope." There were photographs of placard carriers, an angry and vehement crowd of intense, troubled, involved people . . . including many mothers of addicts. The placards read: MAD—MOTHERS AGAINST DRUGS. Opposite all of this was a full-page ad showing a picture of a pack of Kools standing in lush green grass with pretty yellow flowers around it.

The "War on Dope" article continued in full indignation. Opposite a later page of it was a full-page ad stating: "How do you make a better cigarette?—Tareyton's." The "War on Dope" then had the mothers meeting in an active drug fight; opposite them was a full-page ad of Seagram's 100 Pipers Scotch Whisky. The drug war continued with former narcotic addicts helping in the fight against drug addiction. Opposite was a full-page ad in color of Taylor's Champagne.

This apposition of the drug ads (nicotine, alcohol) and the fight against drugs is wild—"he drugs me, he drugs me not, he drugs me, he drugs me not, he drugs me . . . he drugs me . . . he drugs me . . ." and so on, with all the hypnotic power of the incessant barrage, in full color, of the drug appeal. I know this all sounds like an exaggeration—but it is not.

And how about someone starting a group called MADA—Mothers Against Drug Advertising? In fact, how about knocking out advertising altogether?—for,

> if the billboards never fall
> I'll never see a tree at all.

Let's get so we can see some trees, for God's sake!

And—if you think popular magazines are bad, just take a gander at medical magazines! *Wow!*

An article headlined in a medical newspaper reads:

> "AMA emphasizes that MDs
> do not rely only on drug ads"

Methinks they do protest too much!

Tranquillity—tranquillity, like happiness, is something achieved through intricate inner and outer processes, through fighting and grappling and growing toward self and outer awareness, an achievement through overcoming in the Nietzschean sense . . . a dedication and enlightenment in the Buddhist sense reached through great effort and devotion.

And here comes American burlesque in the form of the team of medicos and pharmaceutical companies offering it for merely a price and a swallow! Step up, ladies and gents, for a price and a swallow you enter the stage of enlightenment and tranquillity. No work entailed . . . just pays your money and takes your tranquillity pill.

Hey, suckers, don't you see that tranquilizers have *nothing* to do with tranquillity but rather with death? One more door closed on your life force, bottled up, stifled, smothered, in total subjugation.

Wake up—let your anxieties roam—they *may* lead you home. How can I convince you? I see you are not listening—I see you at your medicine chest reaching for your aspirins, your barbiturates, your Miltowns—how can I shake some life into you . . . some awareness so you can *feel* the disgust at your encouraging your own decay . . . smell the stench of the immoral wasting of your aliveness. Can you right now just be still a moment, feel your own torment, your manifold anxieties, and stay with them . . . hold on to them as to your joys . . . experience them . . . be *real* . . . be an "is" instead of a "should" . . . please don't zombie-ize, don't puppetize, don't robotize, don't vegetabilize yourself with the nearest drug. Your life's blood oozing out is too dear a price to pay for anesthetizing your brain against its pain. Clasp your pain . . . it will lead to your joy.

2

DANGER!
DOCTORS
AT WORK

I guess I could put all my attitudes toward doctors in a few nutshells, like: they're people like anyone else . . . neither you nor I know anyone who is perfect or infallible . . . most doctors don't act as if they make mistakes and they've got a great vocabulary for covering up their ignorance as well as their errors . . . and the ones who hide their ignorance and errors even from themselves are the most dangerous.

How did I ever get involved with doctors and medicine anyway? The first contact with doctors I have any recollection of were those of the clinic variety . . . the outpatient department type . . . at a hospital in Philadelphia. The hospital was several miles from my home . . . and my mother used to walk us there. Wow, what energy she had, all overbrimming five feet of her, with her rapid stride . . . everyone knew, without looking, that Ethel was walking down the street, hearing her energetic footsteps clacking along the sidewalk to the corner grocery or candy store . . . and what energy we had to have to keep up with her as she dragged our little legs over the long distance to the hospital for our colds, flat feet—over that long distance because money was not for luxuries like buses or trolley cars. As I think back now . . . I don't remember the doctors themselves—they were all nondescript except for the ENT (ear, nose, and throat) doctors who always seemed to be old, and the orthopedic doctors who always seemed to be young and strong—but rather what they did . . . the icky times when we'd get a thick-blackish-evil-smelling-liquid argyrol dabbed down our gagging throats by the taciturn old ENT doctors (the panacea at that time for sore throats and the elusive cold) . . . the relatively fun times when we had our flat feet examined for nonexistent progress . . . (we all have flat feet in our family—functional, strong, good-old-fashioned flat feet that can take me through miles of countryside or city blocks but not five minutes in any one of today's stylish heeled shoes—I'm resigned to flat-heeled Dr. Scholl's sandals for the rest of my days) . . . the fun of being shown how to pick up marbles with our toes and walk on the sides of our feet on slanting boards . . . and the drag of having to go downtown to buy heavy, arched oxfords the orthopedists always prescribed and which cost even more than my father's shoes . . . and we were only five and six and seven years old (my older two brothers and I . . . by the time my younger brother was born we either had more bread or we were all healthier because I don't recall those hauls to the hospital after that—maybe we even rebelled).

But most of all, even more than the icky argyrol, I recall the interminable waiting in the hospital's dingy waiting room . . . waiting on hard dark brown benches in a dark room with dark, old-fashioned, stern, dead-looking faces staring down at us (hospital benefactors in old-style clothes on dark canvases . . . as if they posed right there in the dingy waiting room) . . . and over all, the pervasive ether, alcohol, or whatever those other threatening smells were . . . and the interminable waiting . . . waiting . . . waiting . . . and the shame and degradation felt in the sob stories to the social or welfare worker—we always had to report to her first and wait there while my mother cried and told her how poor we were and how we couldn't pay the clinic fee. I feel the sorrow now, my eyes filling with tears as I write this, the torment of those encounters, and the frustration . . . and now the anger that these conditions still exist for so many people in America— for so many adults and children . . . so much degradation and shame just to get some medical attention that should be freely given to all who need it without the cost of a single tear! Any decent society should make it my *right* to be given good medical attention, not my *shame*.

Clinic lines . . . they've gotten longer over the years, with the endless waitings in hospitals with indifferent doctors and nurses who show total disregard for the dignity of the ill person. If you're poor, you're a herd animal . . . and you wait with the herd in humiliation. Ironically, if you're middle-class rich and go to a machine doctor's private office, while you're not humiliated, you still wait. Machinery is machinery, no matter what class it treats.

My next contact with doctors was the medical faculty type. I went to a northern medical college . . . the dean was a southern woman doctor as were a good many of the professors. In those days (1946) most medical colleges had a ½ to 2 percent admission of Jewish male students, less of Jewish women, and even less of black students. This college accepted 35 percent Jews, an unprecedented statistic in the days when Columbia University Medical School was said to have a quota of 1 percent. However, to counterbalance this seeming lack of bias (probably a large portion of their funds came from Jewish people, hence it was good business to keep accepting so many Jews) . . . they had but one black student admitted each year. The trick, even with this stingy statistic, was that they usually managed to flunk out the black student at the end of the first or second year. But I was not to learn of this until considerably later.

In my first year class there was a young black woman . . . I'll call her Jacqueline . . . who had graduated cum laude from Fisk University. She was done in by two professors, both southerners, who flunked her at the end of the first year and then told her to take up nursing at Mercy Hospital, an all black hospital . . . obviously intimating: hey, nigger, stick with your own kind . . . niggers can't be *doctors*—a nurse is good enough for you to be . . . stay with your own people and don't sully us. . . . "If you're black, get back, get back, get back, get back. . . ."

Jesus, I can still see those hounds of southern professors who performed Jacqueline's professional execution—one of them was fat with a bulldog face . . . and the other—a gray-haired stick carrying umbrellas to school on sunny days because "Mama thought it would rain and insisted on it." This is a true quote, I swear. I was riding up in the elevator in school with her this one sunny morning and in her cracked high voice, which would have disappeared if it got any thinner and which all the king's men and the king himself couldn't put together again, she said: "I didn't want to take the umbrella . . . I knew it wouldn't rain, but Mama thought it would rain and insisted on it." "Mama" must have been eighty at least!

Hey, and now that I think of those two insufferable maiden southern unrung belles—could there have been some tie between them other than their common hatred of blacks? Well, what they do in their private lives and any way they choose to do it is their own affair—and has nothing to do with me. But when they violate the education of a black or any other costudent, I am involved—they invite my involvement. The psychic-spiritual-intellectual rape of one student violates all. But I didn't really learn about the school's past history of not-so-subtle discrimination against black students until the second year when a black student, who transferred from a southern medical school, entered my sophomore class . . . I'll call her Doris. She, I, and a white student, whom I shall call Sylvia, studied together. By the way, Sylvia's father owned a newspaper and her mother was an heiress . . . and I used to admire the way she would wear her socks with holes in the back in full view. Because of my own struggling-with-poverty background, a hole in my sock was a personal disgrace and at great discomfort I'd be forever stuffing the hole part of my socks down into my shoes out of view, walking on lumps the rest of the day. How I admired those daring,

34

dashing holes glaring at me from the back of Sylvia's socks—full-blown holes like roses, proud and decorous.

Sylvia's father's newspaper was a "liberal" one, fighting for Henry Wallace and other such liberals . . . he brought up his daughter to dig labor unions, workers' rights, and minority privileges, that is, in *theory.* So what does Sylvia do but fall in love with a black guy, who later becomes a sociologist with a doctorate . . . and Sylvia's husband. What a horrendous breaking apart that started— Sylvia's mother disowned her, her "liberal" father stayed on the mother's side of the conflictful fence . . . and Sylvia found herself with a husband and no parents in one fell swoop.

People just can't stand to face the logical extension (or should I say the human extension) of their preachments! Like . . . our very preachments, carried to their logical conclusions, become our rebellious children. Is this why Freud disowned Wilhelm Reich . . . why liberals disown the Panthers . . . and why parents "explaining" the birds and the bees disown their children's sexuality? The hypocrisy runs rampant. Nobody wants to see the whole story through.

OK—we did our studying together . . . one struggling black, Doris . . . one rich white heiress, Sylvia . . . one Jewish poor white, me. My own relationship with Doris was never an easy one— I always felt I had to prove my loyalty to her and could never fully succeed . . . she seemed always to let me know that she had spent ten years scrubbing floors for Jewish women as their "schwartze" in order to get the bread together for medical school . . . and I don't think I ever fully made it with her—the scars were too deep and I was still always lumped with those Jewish broads who robotized and dehumanized her into a "schwartze" floor scrubber. Look—it's not the floor scrubbing in itself that dehumanizes . . . at times my five-year-old daughter washed my kitchen floor in great pride (put them to work early, yeah! . . . but that's a whole other subject) . . . and I sure felt my humanity when my mother interrupted my stardom at age seven and eight smack in the middle of the plays I was producing with and for the neighborhood kids in our garage, interrupted to make me scrub the kitchen floor . . . no, it's not the activity itself that's degrading . . . it's the *attitude* . . . the *feeling* . . . that's where it's at. When I hear the word "schwartze" coming out of a Jewish mouth, I hear the word "kike" coming out of a Christian mouth . . . and from here, a little one-syllable word, it's a short, short trip to a concentration camp and annihilation.

Wake up, America—this is the 1970's—you gotta start changing your *vocabulary!*

Back to our studying together. In the sophomore year there was this pathology professor from Georgia whom I liked . . . I've always had a thing about devotion to a field, no matter almost what that field is . . . (I can fall in love just hearing about an English teacher, for example, who digs his work and takes it seriously, like life—in fact, isn't work life?) . . . and this prof really dug her work and had an intense interest in teaching the subject, every cell and particle of it. She might have dreamed about making love to dead tissue at night, so intense was her love for the subject. (Hey! She was also a spinster—damn! what was going on in that school anyway?)

However, it began to strike the three of us as dismally curious that Doris was flunking her exams consistently while Sylvia and I were consistently passing, even though we each wrote more or less the same stuff on our exam papers and were equally well prepared. It was then that Sylvia and I began to get suspicious of some dirty work, and we started our private investigations. We learned that as far back as twenty years the school had had the same policy . . . a black graduate of twenty years previously told us she had had to repeat a year . . . some blacks through the years had gotten through by passing for white . . . but most were flunked out at the end of the first or second year. With the results of our investigations and our exam papers to show the actual bias in grading, we went to the NAACP and spread the word around. The school was in a furor . . . the pathology professor and the dean (another southern spinster now that I come to think about it!) held a meeting of the entire school body in which the professor said in her slow Georgian drawl with words that burned marks ón my brain and will never go away: "Some students in mah class accused me of bein preh-judiced . . . Ah want you all to know Ah have no preh-judice . . . Ah was brought up by a Nigra mammy and Ah loved mah Nigra mammy." Most of the students, even the "liberal" ones . . . or perhaps especially the "liberal" ones . . . rallied to her defense . . . she was, after all, an excellent teacher and didn't bother the Jewish "liberal" students . . . her attack was concentrated only on the blacks who got through the first line of defense handled by the southern professors in the first-year class.

Well—after that the heat was on me. Sylvia escaped somehow . . . her father was powerful . . . her mother, an heiress . . . she had a quiet soft-spoken personality and was not obviously a troublemaker . . . and, perhaps above all, she was a White-Anglo-Saxon-Protestant. I, on the other hand, was an odd one—on a four-year scholarship . . . my father, a laborer . . . and I never wore makeup in those days like most of the other girls . . . my hair still in long braids . . . never wore silk stockings and always wore flat-heeled oxfords with bobby socks . . . very much out of step with the stylish well-dressed, well-groomed girls who played bridge in their spare time and were so very ladylike. And . . . besides being in medical school only because of my interest in psychiatry and for no other reason (spending as little time as possible on my medical studies and as much time as possible reading Freud and all the others, and attending all the psychiatric meetings in the city), I spent several evenings a week, in the first year at least, acting in little theatre groups, an interest that was not easy to release from my bloodstream and that often conflicted directly with my medical studies . . . (and which, to this day, still infects my bloodstream).

Somehow, though, I passed the second year . . . Doris was flunked . . . (near the deadline hours, with the NAACP ready to blast the school and open the whole garbage heap to public scrutiny using the three of us as prime witnesses along with our exam papers, Doris backed down—she was afraid this step would jeopardize her medical career and she also feared she would be putting her neck in the noose only for the aggrandizement of the political power of the head of the Philadelphia NAACP. Doris ultimately went to Europe to complete her medical schooling and returned to practice medicine in New York.)

And then I realized . . . it's do or die as a medical student. I was really scared! I felt the hostilities of many of the professors, in particular the southern ones. I began to make a valiant effort to be as inconspicuous as possible . . . started to wear stockings and pay more attention to conforming in appearance and behavior . . . and gave up my work with theatre groups. It was a great strain, but I decided the diploma, the door to my future in psychiatry, was worth the sacrifice . . . the sacrifice was necessary . . . and I did my best to submerge my individuality in that school from that time on.

Damn! Even as I write of those years I find myself now holding my breath, sitting tensely in my chair, trapped by the feeling of the straitjacket I constrained myself in . . . have I ever gotten out of it?—can I have killed so much of my individuality and spontaneity in those years without now having some unresilient scars? As if to prove to myself how free I am, I take a gulp of air—my belly protrudes in Yoga expansion with my inhalation, I roll my head around floppily on my shoulders . . . my body moves freely . . . but still, as I go on . . . or rather back to that time . . . I feel my breath once again constricting . . . my body again getting tight. Dammit! I go off on a rigor mortis head trip when I begin talking about my medical school experience . . . and, while I make some attempts to come back to my present flow, it's not the same. OK, once and for all I'll spit the whole story out and get back to now—the wonderful freedom of now when I can tell the whole damn medical school establishment to go fuck themselves and leave me and the other free-or-trying-to-be-free spirits alone to fly in our own way.

You see what I mean—here, sitting in my "safe" room with my medical diploma somewhere in a pile of papers as an open sesame to freedom in my work and with a sky getting light in the dawn rising over the ocean . . . all I have to do is to think back to those imprisoned times and my flow gets imprisoned back there. See what I mean . . . the past is a killer. Lightning sky, lights over the ocean, cluttered freedom of my room—I embrace you all—I greet you and meet you and shall devote myself to stay in your embrace—in the embrace of my infinite *now,* my forever *now,* my free-breathing *now.*

In the third year of med school the entire clinical staff seemed to know of my attack on the school's racism and they kept watch . . . Big Sister was watching. From having gotten an A in every chemistry course I had taken at the University of Pennsylvania (I was a chem major and English minor . . . my love minor, pragmatic considerations were major) . . . I now began to do mediocre work. And worst of all—I began to lose confidence in myself and my abilities . . . the more self-confidence I lost, the more my performance deteriorated. The cold war was on . . . and I was a frozen stiff. I felt the eyes of the staff always on me . . . how did I ever avoid a full-blown paranoia? . . . and underneath my frozen conformity, my rebellious ardor tormented no one but myself.

At the end of the third year they told me I flunked pediatrics and would have to repeat the exam in the fall after doing some extra work in pediatrics during the summer. Wow—I went limp when I heard this . . . even now I feel the dishrag sinking limpness covering the fear—they had me now! (Hey, I wrote a line some months ago and it's been hanging around on a little piece of paper on my desk waiting till I could find a place for it to lodge . . . and I just did: *fear is the thin veil of ferocity.* Underneath that limp fear did I not have a murderous rage against those damn establishment professors and their power to destroy me? . . . and is that why I went so limp—to protect myself against my own unacceptable ferocity?)

When I heard the news, I suddenly built up a horror picture of spending a summer working under those pediatric professors who had flunked me and who would undoubtedly devise excruciating and sinister tortures for me . . . for were they not part of, as

Kesey describes in *One Flew Over the Cuckoo's Nest,* the Combine? I knew instinctively of the torture chamber they had in mind for me . . . and knew, too, that at the end of the summer they would exterminate me and my entire medical career as they had the two black students before me . . . in their eyes I was another black. The pediatric staff was composed of professors whom the school administration could count on to support its nefarious objectives in general . . . and in my case in particular, knocking me off was *it.*

Even to this day I don't know how justified that failure in pediatrics was. Admittedly I was under constant surveillance of the southern dean . . . but I had to fight against my inner rebellion at having to study stuff that was not my major or even minor interest, and that seemed to bear no relationship at all to my real interests. But, I repeat, I knew instinctively with all the self-preservative urgings of my pores that a summer at the pediatric concentration clinic at the medical school, as the Combine intended, would assuredly knock me off.

Hey . . . something important . . . that surveillance I mentioned before—that Big Sister watching from above . . . putting me below her big-eyed scrutiny . . . enough evil eyes watching me, enough negative vibes pouring into me . . . and they don't even have to lift a finger or falsify exam grades . . . I do the job myself . . . I myself do myself in! . . . I fail all by myself . . . I confuse myself, confound myself, impound myself. For the first time in my life I was in direct contact with the paranoia, based on real externals, that paralyzes its victim first, mesmerizes him into a belief in his inferiority, and then makes him, the victim, become his own executioner. Wow! If I, a white person in that racist school, came so close to failure . . . imagine how strong must be the spirit in those black students who survived even one year in that disemboweling arena conducted by female frustrates.

I suddenly mustered whatever life was left in me—I became a lioness . . . and out of nowhere that I recall . . . thin air? . . . inspiration? . . . fate? . . . just plain desperation and need?

. . . I located a pediatrician in New York City, a professor of pediatrics at a New York medical college . . . a guy who, I figured, would give me an unbiased report and a nontormented summer work experience. I also figured he was sufficiently removed from my medical school and sufficiently connected in a substantial way in New York to pose a threat to any shenanigans on the part of my southern and southern-type professors . . . they wouldn't dare contradict a guy of his standing! Man! That was the cleverest thing I did those entire four years of medical school—it saved my life!

Well, I worked in the pediatrician's office throughout that summer . . . he turned out to be a really neat guy, warm and human . . . but still I kept an awareness of my anxiety about medical school and all my undercurrent rebelliousness—all of which made me act kind of confused and dumb . . . but, nice guy that he was, he overlooked my frequently-erupting *mishegos* (craziness). He wrote an excellent report about my work in his office (did I merit it?), and at the end of the summer I passed my pediatric reexam and was allowed to enter the senior year. Whew! Reprievèd . . . Reprievèd . . . (recall Bertolt Brecht's song in *The Threepenny Opera?*) . . . reprievèd . . . at least for the time being.

The following year was a dungeon of suspense . . . not knowing even on graduation day (they had to get their last drop of blood) whether I'd be finally and fully reprieved by that hunk of paper, the diploma. The graduation exercises were held at the University of Pennsylvania's huge auditorium . . . the procedure entailed having the graduates go up on the stage individually and pass in front of a lineup of professors, one of whom capped each graduate and then the pathology professor, who had flunked Doris for her black skin, handed out the diploma whereupon each graduate was to shake her hand. When I came up to her, my legs shaking and my eyes searching for a yes or no (there were rumors floating around that I would not graduate—oh, torture!), she gave me my diploma . . . and I offered her my hand (yes, I really did!) . . . (listen, she might have grabbed that diploma right out of my tight sweaty clutch!) . . . and she made a scowling face and hissed at

41

me—right there in front of those thousands of people watching, so deep was her venom . . . and she never did offer her hand.

But, yeah! . . . I had the paper in my hand . . . in my hand was that open sesame to the door of psychiatry and worth all the blood I had poured out for it. But . . . it took me several years to get rid of the anemia, to fill out the squashed parts of my personality that I had ironed so flat those last two years at medical school. And now, finally and at long long last, here and now, I'm back to not wearing stockings (except on cold days) and to wearing sandals most of the time (or what would be the use of living in Miami?) . . . and to saying what I feel . . . and getting more and more to feeling what I say.

What a long road home! . . . And I almost didn't make it whole . . . or did I? I look out at the waves grinding, pounding— vibrate somewhat with their knocking on the shoreline—and feel together and whole. I lose it—this wholeness—whenever I go back to my torture chamber . . . to those gauleiters of my spontaneity and uniqueness—to those held-in breathless last two years of medical school . . . or to any time away from the glorious tune of my present vibrations.

So—good-bye to my alma mater . . . and good-bye to you, my Georgian professor of pathology . . . you're dead now and you can't snarl at any radical uniquenesses anymore nor threaten them or their black sisters' medical diplomas . . . but weirdly enough, I always admired you for your devotion to your subject. It's that hang-up of mine. Through all the bitterness and frustration of those years at medical school after I hurled the gauntlet down before your white racism, a part of me had to admire and respect not your lack of humanity but your single-minded love of the study of pathology and your meticulous, loving teaching of this subject to all except the black students you feared and despised. Good-bye, you poor pure scientist . . . split off from your own person . . . there was more personness in the little fingernail of your Nigra Mammy than you could ever know in your autopsies, your microscopic study of dead tissue on dead slides in a dead world of dead white purity and southern white women medical professors. Rest in peace.

My internship was uneventful . . . except that my verree bourgeois fellow interns and residents (with a few delightful exceptions) considered as peculiar my interest in reading French poetry and some works in French by Piaget . . . instead of concerning myself with the business aspects of medicine that so absorbed them. The hospital establishment and my colleagues did not know of my hitchhiking trips to and from Philadelphia to visit my family (my salary was $35 a month) and my trips via thumb to Red Bank to visit my therapist weekly. Had they known, I would have fared no better in social ostracism than I had at medical school. I was learning to conceal my differences and uniqueness from the members of the Medical Club.

The most astonishing thing I learned in my internship was that doctors perform operations for *nonmedical, nonhealth reasons!* I recall my distress not only with the gynecologist on our staff who notoriously removed all women's wombs he could get his hands on, but with the nonchalant way the gynecology residents joked about Dr. Otto and his hatchery. In the operating room, while cutting into the woman's flesh, he would crack "dirty" jokes and expect the residents to laugh and the nurses to blush. Something in the way he handled the woman's flesh bespoke his contempt. Somehow my horrification was out of step with those businessmen residents who planned to follow in Dr. Otto's lucrative footsteps. Yes, my internship provided a rude, crude initiation into the realities of the Fraternal Order of Caduceus!

My next distressing personal contact with nonpsychiatric doctors occurred years later when I came to a southern state. After practicing in New York and California, having gotten medical licenses in these two states, I had to take a basic science exam and a state medical board exam to get a license in South State. I passed the basic science exam and then was eligible to take the medical exams, but I was not given permission to take them as were the others who

43

passed. The local office of the South Board of Medical Examiners kept putting me off, saying they couldn't yet grant me permission but didn't tell me why, and I was sitting on tenterhooks, getting more and more paranoid about the situation. Finally, not long before the date the exams were scheduled, I received the following letter on the official stationery of the South State Board of Medical Examiners:

June 20, 1968

Dear Dr. Walkenstein:

Please be informed that your application to take the written examinations for medical licensure has been received.

Upon inquiry into your background and qualifications, it has been revealed that at one time you were a proponent of the principles of orgonomy and the use of the Orgone Accumulators in psychiatry.

Because there is doubt as to the validity of these principles at this point in the practice of medicine, your application to take the written examinations must be approved by the entire medical board. You may therefore appear before the board at 10 A.M., Thursday, July 3, 1968, at the Danbury Hotel.

Should the medical board not be fully satisfied with your credentials, it may develop that you will not be allowed to take the medical examinations now scheduled for July 5, 6, 7, 1968, and you may require a further hearing to more fully investigate this matter.

Sincerely yours,

Steven Barton, M.D.
Executive Director

I was not to know until less than twenty-four hours before the exams whether or not I would be permitted to take them. (Try studying under these conditions!) But at least the mystery as to my failure to receive permission to take the exams was cleared up and I could put to rest all the paranoid doubts and wonderments as to what, in my tortuous past, was creating my present obstacle. Yet, I was still in potential danger: the founder of orgonomy, Dr. Wilhelm Reich (a brilliant physician whose book, *Character Analysis,* can be found on most analysts' shelves today), had been thrown in jail and his books burned by the federal government. During my internship in 1951 I had attended a regular series of case seminars presented by a group of physicians who met to discuss Reich's works and the therapeutic results they achieved in using his techniques. At that time Reich was still in jail facing a court hearing, and along with the others in the group I signed a paper presented by Reich's lawyer to the court to the effect that from my medical experience I believed in the efficacy of Reich's therapeutic approach.

It wasn't until I appeared before the large group of South Medical Board examiners, sitting augustly around long wide tables—some eighteen or so doctors—that I heard about this long forgotten paper I had signed some seventeen years previously.

I don't like going back to that board hearing . . . to that room with the heavy, wide tables separating the members of the group from one another and all of them from me . . . but I feel I must, with you, face my ordeal. One red-necked physician with a thick southern accent kept needling me . . . was he bothered by my being a woman physician and a Jewish one at that? . . . or did I seem black to him? Actually, none of them seemed to have heard of Wilhelm Reich, but some of them had vaguely heard of the "sex box," as one of them satirically stated with a pornographic twisted smile. Some of them came to my defense (I was very "nice" to all of them—even the red-necked cracker) and pointed out I had signed that paper in my internship, implying that I didn't know much then. Encouraged by their softening attitude, I told them I was surprised to be having this hearing about a group I belonged to in New York in 1951, and that since then I had worked for various clinics, the Veterans Administration Hospital, the New York City Board of Education, and had received medical licenses in New York and

45

California without any difficulty and had never been questioned. One of them proudly said: "In South State we're thorough!" He seemed annoyed that I would question the validity of this hearing. After many grueling questions, they finally ended by telling me to be sure not to sign any more papers. The red-necked guy was still expostulating: "How do we know she won't sign any more papers like that?" . . . to which I answered sweetly: "I've learned something since my internship days." Many of them by this time were smiling in relief—they were reluctant witch-hunters after all and seemed glad to end my ordeal. Throughout the meeting I kept to what I thought was a high level of medical and scientific accuracy in describing as best I could Reich's works of a lifetime in a few short statements. I was struck, on another level, with the desire of many of these men to hear some lascivious details of my Reich experience. I left them frustrated. As I was leaving the room, one of them laughingly said something about the box and, as the door closed behind me, the general laughter in the room became raucous. They agreed to accept me as a candidate, and I went on to complete my South State medical board examinations successfully. Reprieved again from the hungry maw of the Caduceus Wearers.

My own father was hair-raisingly almost not reprieved. Now, he's always been a great storyteller, bringing us up on stories of Russia, folk myths, the old lady without an arm, tales of Hershel Shteploya . . . great stories, mixed with recollections of his childhood experiences helping a magician in his act, playing mandolin and balalaika with Dave Apollon in Kiev, getting his gang to strike back at the anti-Semitic hoods who ran rampant in Kiev, and on and on.

And while we're on it, a favorite story about Hershel shouldn't be overlooked, no?

Hershel was the Russian Charlie Chaplin—champion of the poor little guy—a poor Jewish fellow who somehow always got the better of the rich and the non-Jew (often synonymous with rich) . . . in short, a Jewish folk hero. As my Dad tells the story, Hershel borrowed from his neighbor, a wealthy farmer and landowner, a big plate . . . (get the Yiddish inflection?—it's part of the story and

46

you gotta say it right to get the right effect, of course). After a while, Hershel brought him back the big plate and a half dozen little ones and told him it gave birth to the little ones—so the farmer thought he was a very honest guy—so he said he could borrow anything else he ever needed. So—a little while later, Hershel came back to the rich farmer and said he was having a big shindig and wondered if he could borrow a samovar—so the farmer loaned him the biggest one, figuring maybe he'd get little samovars—so Hershel kept it for a long time and finally the farmer decided to go over and see what was wrong. When Hershel saw him coming, he hurried up and took his shoes off and sat down on the floor and got his wife to do the same. When the farmer came in and saw him on the floor, he knew there was a death in the family (the Jewish ritual of "sitting shiva") and he said: "What happened?" and Hershel said: "You know, the poor samovar died." "How can a samovar die?" asked the farmer, and Hershel answered: "The same way as a big dish can have babies." . . . (Wow!—you could almost write a whole psychosociological study of the Jew based on this story alone! . . . by their heroes so shall ye know them?)

Back to my Dad and his "close shave." When I was in my internship in New York, my father developed an inguinal hernia and I located a good surgeon for him in his hometown, Philadelphia. After he was operated on, I called him from New York prior to visiting him at the hospital that weekend. He said they had begun to shave his head while he was in the operating room, mistaking him for another patient. The story was so ludicrous that I thought it was an exaggeration for the sake of humor—just one more of my Dad's stories.

When I arrived in his hospital room directly from New York, he was sitting up in bed and my heart took a leap—there across his scalp was a two-inch line of shaved head furrowed from his forehead to the back of his head. I suddenly had the fearful flash that maybe he did have brain surgery after all and that he wanted to spare me the worrisome news. And then his story unfolded: on the operative morning he was wheeled down the hall where, outside the

47

operating room, was another patient on a stretcher; a hospital chart was placed at the foot of each stretcher. My father was wheeled into the O.R. and the nurse placed a razor at his forehead and shaved a furrow to the back of his neck. At first he thought the head shaving had something to do with the administering of the anesthesia, but after a few more excursions of the razor this thought seemed somehow too farfetched to him—so he said, hesitantly: "Uh, pardon me, nurse—but could you tell me what shaving my head has to do with my hernia operation?" He said the nurse turned pale, began to shake, checked his chart, and then got all confused. She had mixed his chart with the other patient's who was scheduled for brain surgery! Had he not spoken up at that crucial moment, what with a mask on his face and being anesthetized, it is likely that the surgeon would not have recognized the error—and his brain would have gone under the knife. He talked to the doctor about it later and he was told that the doctor would have recognized him—but none of us swallowed that!

Hey!—have you spoken up today? *Don't take anything for granted, dammit* . . . especially if you're in a hospital . . . Speak Up! . . . shout, yell, scream . . . protect yourself . . . for the protectors won't, and don't ever forget this . . . you, yourself, must be your own protector!

Even being a doctor or a member of his family is no shield against the manifold "errors" (abuses?) performed by the Medical Club. One night I phoned some friends—a doctor and his wife. They are atypical of the average established medical couple in that they are ideologically rebellious against the abuses in the status quo . . . a hangover from their fringy have-not days . . . and give eloquent lip service to their ideals . . . they are both highly literate and articulate . . . while keeping an active foothold—I should say handhold—on the favors of the establishment. Thus, they straddle both worlds and are not too comfortable in either one. At any rate, my doctor friend answered the phone and told me he had received horrible news that his father had just died in a New York hospital

48

and that a doctor had killed him. Two weeks previously his father had gone to the emergency room of Cole Hospital and the doctor on duty examined his abdomen, which was distended and rigid, and decided it was just a fecal impaction in a seventy-six-year-old man . . . (in my internship I came across, for the first time, the word "crock"—generally used by doctors in training to describe older patients . . . which was a way of warding off any serious concern about them as people) . . . so the doctor gave the seventy-six-year-old "crock" an enema and sent him home. Actually, my friend's father had an obstruction caused by a slight herniation of the gut. The enema caused a perforation in his bowel with subsequent widespread peritonitis. After five days he was hospitalized; the proper diagnosis was made and surgically corrected. He was given huge doses of antibiotics . . . but the assault on his organism from the peritonitis was too much to bear and he died.

And the doctor in that emergency room . . . how many more people, young and old, will he kill . . . how many in your family and mine? Who pays the price for such haphazard ignorance? You do . . . I do. Beware of your physician's counsel . . . taste it well . . . chew it well . . . before *you* decide to swallow it. And be sure you know how to vomit it up and look for other tastes before you open a receptive mouth. Your life is at stake. Are you anxious? Good! . . . this anxiety might save your life!

In every major city there are gynecologists who have the sub rosa reputation among doctors of removing all uteri they can manage to get hold of . . . the hatchet man in my internship was not at all unique . . . it's almost an aphorism that if surgeons were women there would be a radical decline in the incidence of hysterectomies. And if the profit motive were removed—what a precipitous drop! As for appendectomies, a surgeon (again, in my internship . . . see how valuable an initiation rite this internship is?) told me that if, on operation for the alleged appendicitis, the appendix looks normal, "all you have to do prior to cutting it out is to rub it between your thumb and forefinger and it will become sufficiently inflamed that

49

the subsequent pathology report will read 'Acute Inflammation.' This way you can't be held responsible for operating on a normal appendix."

Oh, you Dealers in Human Flesh . . . who not only get your pound of flesh but your coffers filled therewith. What will you do when we flesh bearers become proud and wary and start to respect our own flesh more than your coffers? It is not the honest mistakes you bury that infuriate me . . . it is the audacity with which you contemptuously and nefariously mangle our human flesh for your own psychic and material ends.

I reach an impasse when I try to put into words my wordless sensations of impatience, disgust, outrage at the death-dealing flesh dealers. Whenever I feel it's no use—I can't really say meaningfully or movingly what I'm digging at—when I feel like closing my note-book and giving up, I get some fresh impetus to impart these things and share my feelings with you. This time it was in the guise of a telephone call I received early one morning from a patient whose husband, Bert, was in a hospital recuperating from a simple herniorrhaphy. She said Bert had told his surgeon about his prostate condition prior to the operation. Typically, the surgeon wasn't listening and did not take proper precautions. Postoperatively Bert developed a spiking fever of 105 degrees and an acute urinary blockage, whereupon the surgeon balled Bert out for not mentioning the prostate condition sooner! All the surgeon had had to do, actually, was to have opened his ears and listened. But who listens? The impertinence of the guy—immediately shifting the blame to his patient. Damn these prima donnas—I can tolerate their histrionics on the stage of the Metropolitan Opera House, but I'll be damned if I want them wielding their dramatics on my flesh in the operating room!

I leave the operating room prima donnas to their hysterics, pray that not too many patients fall prey to them, and go on to other doctors and their alleged, exalted glory. Some time ago a friend and former patient, Lynne, called to tell me of some lower abdominal pains and other gynecological complaints and to ask me if I knew a good gynecologist. I had no personal referral to give her, but I mentioned that Edith, a friend of hers whom she had referred to me for treatment, was going to Dr. Palm who had a big reputation at one of the largest local hospitals. Also, Edith's husband, a medical student, chose Dr. Palm for her because of the high reputation he had among doctors in the medical school. So Lynne went to him for a few visits . . . on the third visit she was told she had a dermoid cyst of the ovary (no X ray was taken!) and she would have to be operated upon. In the meantime I had suggested another doctor for consultation and this time we both had heard independently of this second gynecologist's "fine" reputation, and Lynne went also to him. He examined her cursorily, said she had some vaginal inflammation, and without taking a smear (!) gave her some oral antibiotics and some other medication. This sounded like poor medicine to me, and she was still worried about the dermoid cyst and the impending operation (the second doctor said nothing about a mass behind the uterus) so I called a good general practitioner I know—a man of integrity who has concern for his patients—and he recommended a *third* gynecologist. This third doctor, Dr. Season, was astonished that the first doctor diagnosed a dermoid cyst without an X ray and that the second prescribed antibiotic medication without proper diagnosis. Dr. Season not only gave her a thorough examination but was also magnificently human in response to her. When he examined her breasts (she was a young, seven-year-long married woman) he commented that she'd have no trouble nursing her babies (wow!—what doctor thinks positive like this, much less encouraging nursing these days!), and while he was examining her pelvis he told her the dimensions were good for easy delivery of babies (another wow!—no scary bubbeh-meisehs—old wives' tales— from this human being worthy of his title)—also he said there was no evidence of a cyst or any other growth, that her vagina and cervix were clear, and he could discover no pathology! (Another uterus or ovary rescued from the butcher's knife.) When next I saw my patient, Edith, I told her I had some bad news about her gynecologist and that I would recommend she try Dr. Season when next she needed a gynecological exam. I told her I didn't want to take the

51

time in her session and that she could call Lynne who would give her the details. She said she was surprised because Dr. Palm had a fine reputation and that, in fact, a friend of hers was going to have a hysterectomy for fibroids. I gave her Dr. Season's name on my prescription pad and told her to talk to Lynne first and then, if she was convinced, to do her friend a favor and recommend she go for a consultation. The following week I got the follow-up: Edith's friend, a young woman in her twenties, scheduled to have her uterus removed by Dr. Palm for alleged fibroids, was examined by Dr. Season, who by the way was chief of service in gynecology and obstetrics at one of the local hospitals, and was found normal in every respect and with no indication for a hysterectomy *whatsoever*.

So—Lynne and Edith's friend were both reprieved—by a hairsbreadth—from the hands of the belly cutters. Lynne went on, the following year, to have a healthy baby—the natural way without anesthetizing drugs.

Dammit!—will we ever learn to question authority—medical and otherwise?

Question: What's wrong with questioning?

Answer: It creates anxiety.

Question and Answer: Great! If you're anxious about your flesh, you'll do something to protect it. Be Anxious? Yes, Be Anxious! Question—be anxious—doubt—be anxious—compare—resist—desist—question—doubt—be anxious—protect—spare your flesh—resist his "feelings"—don't cop out on yourself—resist—doubt—question—be anxious—stay anxious—stay *alive!*

Before we leave the womb doctors, I'd like to tell you of a doctor's middle-aged wife, tense and extremely anxious, mother of three grown children, who came to see me in great distress. She was pregnant and felt she couldn't-wouldn't survive another pregnancy and that she was ready to kill herself if necessary to avoid this. Another psychiatrist had advised abortion in order to conserve her life and I concurred, giving her thus the two psychiatric recommendations required by state law to legitimize a D & C (dilatation and curettage) to remove the fertilized egg from the uterus . . . a simple scraping procedure.

With the two written recommendations, she went to a gynecologist recommended by her physician-husband. The gynecologist told her he'd take it up with the board at his hospital and felt it would go through, but he warned her that "in cases like yours I always do a hysterectomy!" He had suddenly become God, punishing her for being pregnant and for wanting an abortion on top of it! In her already depressed, shaken state she was all but pushed to the brink by this doctor's brutality and inhuman threat.

Where are we going to find the doctor we can, in all ways, trust? So rare is he that, including myself, he is virtually nonexistent. We pay the penalty whenever we give our own judgment over completely to someone else. There just is no God walking the earth . . . neither in the form of doctor or any other shape. There's no help for it but to keep our own judgment somehow alive and listen to its voice . . . judgment day is every day and it is we, ourselves, who must sit on the throne.

Any Medical Club member who goes his individual way finds first ostracism . . . and then annihilation. To contradict the "group" is asking for it. In medicine they elevate this lowly rule to the level of ethical considerations: ethics bind my tongue and don't permit my speaking out against surgeons who cut flesh without cause, gynecologists who rip out intact and healthy uteri, optometrists who give glasses to kids with normal vision—that is, normal before the optometrist begins to "work" on them, dentists who, without proper cause, prescribe exorbitant and radical gum treatment to kids of gullible parents . . . I have committed the unethical crime of resisting this, I admit . . . I have unethically denounced the doctors who threatened to do these things to my patients and I have successfully protected these patients from such brutalization. Fortunately, I was always able to find some rare doctor of integrity to counteract the butchers in whose grasping hands my patients put their lives and their flesh. (Meat workers, please pardon the disparaging comparison.) And—when I told my psychiatric colleagues of my intervening in this way, they almost invariably attacked me for "getting involved" . . . for "creating anxiety."

Here are some results of the anxiety I created by questioning medical authorities:

In my New York practice I had a severely hypochondriacal patient who had run the gamut of physicians before he submitted to the idea that maybe he was psyching himself into his illnesses. When he began treatment with me, he committed himself to the following negotiable contract with me—namely, that he would stay out of doctors' offices unless we both agreed he needed to go. He did well for some weeks and then I had to leave town for a week or two. In my absence he developed severe right upper abdominal pain and went to a surgeon who told him he had an enlarged liver and should go into the hospital for a liver biopsy. In the nick of time I returned; the surgeon refused to discuss the patient's medical situation adequately with me . . . and it smelled fishy. Luckily, I knew a good internist whose competence and integrity I trusted, and I referred the patient to him for consultation. The verdict— *normal*—and another surgeon was defeated in his ensnaring scheme.

A patient told me her teen-age son was diagnosed as having severe dental and gum problems and the dentist said he wanted to do a major job on her son to the tune of $1,500. After having been through a slew of lousy dentists myself, I happened to fall on a honorable dentist who seemed competent—his philosophy was to let the mouth dictate the treatment, following nature's commands and not imposing any needlessly radical treatment. I suggested she take her son to him for a consultation. Result—*normal mouth*— averting the creation of a chronic dental invalid.

An eye doctor was consultant to a school for children with learning disorders where I was also consultant. Having had several personal dealings with eye doctors (my two sons had had surgery for eye muscle imbalance at an early age), I was somewhat hip on the subject. One of my patients, an eight-year-old boy, was told by the eye doctor that he needed corrective lenses and a full series of eye exercises, amounting to around $1,000 in toto. I found this out after his mother had already purchased glasses through the doctor. Fortunately, I knew a terrific eye man and referred the mother with my patient for a consultation. Result—*normal visual-motor function,* no indication for glasses or eye exercises of any kind.

Am I becoming clear? I want to contact you out there, touch you with my ideas, my feelings. I want to move you . . . make you anxious, alive. Yes—my own movement becomes excited when I feel in contact with it and with its propelling you to movement, to change.

I'm eager now to bring us to a confrontation with the medicine man.

Doctors—and their belief in the traditional. Every time I pick up a book that deals with doctors historically I run into the same theme—nothing has changed—doctors are changeless in rejecting the new and in ostracizing, persecuting, and crucifying anyone in or out of their midst who threatens their traditional, secure, boxed-in "knowledge," their body of facts that has been taught them notwithstanding how dead that body lies.

Why are doctors so notoriously reactionary, ever ready to gun down the voice of change, the voice of the future? I think we can find our clue in the roots of doctoring, which hearken back to the early medicine man, his mysticism, his aura, his superstition. Vehement denial of any possible connection with these forebears makes our modern medicine man so ferociously vituperative in his attack on anything beyond the pale of traditional acceptance. Is it his own present quackery he is thus denying? This denial and vituperation reminds me of Ruth Benedict's anthropological study in *Patterns of Culture* of the man captured from his tribe of origin and enslaved in a new tribe and who, in later warfare against his original tribe, becomes the fiercest of warriors.

All deny. When doctors get riled up about quacks and fringy

medical people, they somehow seem to protest too much . . . what is it in themselves they are thus projecting? The very things we most get upset about in others are often the very things, in ourselves, we are attempting to deny and disown. If a doctor were really honest with himself and his patients, he would develop the proper humility about his pharmacopoeia and his skills . . . and his lack of skills . . . he would acknowledge that yesterday's medicine is indeed today's quackery, today's treatment is indeed tomorrow's monster.

I once asked a great and rare pediatrician in Los Angeles, Dr. Spivack, what he thought of the fluoride they were putting in infant vitamin drops and he said: "This year, fine. But I've been in medicine long enough to know that what's accepted today may be harmful tomorrow." A beautiful man!

Do you want to get a doctor's dander up? Just mention intuition! . . . or art! Doctors give lip service to the fact that they "practice the *Art* of Medicine," but if you accuse them of being intuitive, they will holler—"we are men of *Science,* facts not fancies." Remember, it was these men of science who were prescribing thalidomide to thousands of women in Europe . . . and most American doctors would have done likewise except for a fluke.

I *feel* (intuitive?—perhaps, but then, I'm not a scientist and thus am free to follow my intuitive leanings) that today's contraceptive pill with all its damming back of the natural hormonal balance, especially in young women, is the Pandora's box housing tomorrow's monster. When I read of the rise of breast cancer in American women, claiming around thirty-one thousand lives as a leading cause of cancer deaths, my intuitive blame of the contraceptive pill and its pushers peaks a new high. It's a curious paradox that doctors will avoid any new and contradictory approach and at the same time will fall headlong into the arms of the first drug salesman offering his panacean wares . . . the profit-motivated doctor falling for the profit-motivated drug salesman, both speaking the same language.

56

Denial—one of the commonest of man's mental mechanisms. It is so pervasive a phenomenon . . . translated, it means disowning a part of the self . . . and contributes to the general tone of alienation we are experiencing. When I deny my origins, I deny that part of myself connected with my past and that is still alive within me. When I deny a part of myself, I fragment myself, cut myself off from me, and thence feel alienated, isolated, lonely. When I accept me, when I am together with myself, I am synchronized, moving with my aliveness, not lonely. Loneliness has little to do with the presence/absence of other people—it has rather to do with the presence/absence of myself. Am I fully present? . . . all pieces together? . . . then I am not alone—alien—alienated. Am I absent?—is part of me absent?—then I am lonely—lonely in a crowd, alone in a relationship, alienated, separated out—separated from myself.

The alienated doctor is indoctrinated to follow the traditional group, to accept what is handed down to him without questioning. He is forced to join the medical club, the local county medical society, for without membership he is forbidden the "privilege" of hospitalizing his patients. So, merged with the group, the doctor leans on the group and its traditional values for his pseudosecurity. Even his medical practices are dictated by the group, malpractice being defined as that which differs from procedures accepted by the majority of the medical group in that locale (how tight, this holding to traditional practices!).

So, the doctor, clinging to The Club for safety, never gets a chance to go his own way, to move with or even discover his unique individual flow. It is truly the rare, beautiful doctor that can go his own way . . . and he's always certain to be persecuted when he does. The Club won't tolerate lonely eagles.

It was my privilege to meet one of these eagles. A couple of weeks ago I attended a medical seminar on "Current Cancer Concepts" at Mount Sinai Hospital in Miami Beach and was amazed at what I heard there. When I was in medical school over twenty years before, I was taught that the best treatment for breast cancer that had spread to the lymph nodes in the axilla was a radical mastectomy followed by radiation. Not having heard or read to the contrary, I assumed that this treatment was generally accepted today. Much to my surprise, I learned that doctors all over the world have *stopped* using this approach except for doctors in the United States, who continue to use this form of treatment even though it has been demonstrated to *increase* fatalities. Dr. George Crile, Jr., a surgeon with a very fine reputation, was really letting his guts out as he spoke of study after study that proved the increased mortality of the orthodox accepted approach used by most American surgeons today. He almost pleadingly wailed: "We've known of these damaging results for twenty years now and we in America stand unique and alone in the world in using this approach [of radical mastectomy]—in all the rest of the world this procedure has been altered. There is no reason to inflict on women the higher morbidity rate of radical removal of breast and muscles."

He presented a study of a huge number of women with breast cancer—those who went to a general practitioner and had a simple mastectomy (leaving the lymph nodes and muscles intact)—those who went to a board certified surgeon and had a radical mastectomy. The result was a longer survival in those women who were operated on by their general practitioners and had a simple mastectomy.

By this time, Dr. Crile was almost yelling in his emphasis: "Radiation plus radical mastectomy increases morbidity. You couldn't *dream* of a better way of increasing cancer growth than destroying lymphatics as is done in a radical mastectomy plus radiation!"

He ended with the declaration: "We [surgeons] in America, under the influence of Halsted and the universities, have completely failed to keep abreast with changing times and advances in the rest of the world!"

The doctor whose talk followed this, and whom regrettably I did not hear (Dr. Simon Kramer), referred to radical mastectomy as "mutilectomy."

On my way out of the auditorium, I overheard some typical

walled-off, dead-looking doctors commenting about "how fanatic that guy is on this subject—as for myself, I'm not convinced."

Why have American surgeons failed to cease their fatal muti-lectomies? For fear of going off here into all kinds of fanciful and homicidal speculations (do female surgeons really perform less mutilectomies than male surgeons?), I shall leave my questions open for your consideration. But if you have a surgeon who wears any of the depersonalized look of a mutilator, find a doctor worthy of this name, like Dr. Crile, and resist the violator's attempt to mutilate your flesh.

Care for your flesh—be careful of your flesh—pay attention to your flesh.

And don't for a minute think these medical doctors are the only ones who are dangerous—psychiatrists and medical psychoanalysts are doing their share of harm. So—be wary of all types of mutilators —yes, be anxiously wary—dare to care for your own flesh. Remember, "If I care not for myself, who will care for me?"

And to the doctors I say:

But if you care only for yourself (your ego, your bankroll) what are you?

3

DEAD MEN
IN A DEADLY ART

Being a psychiatrist or medical psychoanalyst does not in itself equip a person to deal with human problems. In fact, considering the long years of rigid schooling and training required to come by these titles (sixteen years of premedical schooling, four years of medical school, one or two years of internship, three years of psychiatric residency, plus elective psychoanalytic schooling), I would say that the holding of such titles by a person acts rather as a deterrent to his ability to work with and relate to other persons. So, being himself hampered in simply feeling by the rigors and rigidities of his training, he is little equipped to give the emotional nourishment necessary for growth in his patient.

None of my psychiatric and psychoanalytic preceptors ever spoke of how little they knew and how much there was to discover. No one ever made the comment: "We are ignorant men groping toward the light." Over the years I have come to see this statement as the truest that one can make in our present state of knowledge of the functioning of the human personality. While we have made some slight inroads, we are still engaged in a Lilliputian battle, and anyone who sets forth a dogma presuming to have The Answer is doomed to remain in ignorance.

What shits most psychiatrists are! Most of them are robotized businessmen on ego trips, supporting their vested interests and properties on the patient's blood, steeping themselves in the security of traditional "knowledge," not exposing themselves to any new or potentially threatening ideas, and, above all, never exposing their humanity, their human frailties, or passions to their patients but rather staying as tin-untouchable Gods. And the incredible rationalizations and maneuverings to keep their God-armor shined up!

If I've maligned any real-people psychiatrists by lumping them with the thousands of rigor mortis shrinks in America, I wish they'd step forward . . . I'd like to meet them. I've already met several in a group called the American Academy of Psychotherapists, which does seem to have a run on real-people professionals (who let their real or symbolic long hair down in a journal called *Voices*). As for the thousands remaining, do they dare greet me after hearing my dissent? There are so few among them that I can truly trust and respect. One man does come to mind just now, a psychiatrist with decency and integrity . . . a man who doesn't use his patients for his own material or ego ends. He never takes on a patient he feels he can't help . . . and he doesn't play God. When he referred a patient to me he said: "I'm getting tired and you're enthusiastic . . . and she's a tough case. I think you could do a better job with her than I." And he told the patient the same thing! That really knocked me out. What do you think of *that* for integrity! Hey, psychiatrists—how many of you can make a statement like that to one of your colleagues . . . or to your patients? How many of you have made such statements? When I get tired I hope I'll be honest enough to make such a statement. I hope I'm honest enough now. Goddamn—how rare is the man of truth—and how beautiful! Dr. Cantor, I bow before you.

I'd like to tell you of an experience I had with a group of psychiatrists—members of a psychiatric association I belonged to. The locale is irrelevant . . . the more than fourteen thousand psychiatrists in this country do not differ so much from city to city . . . no one city has a monopoly on the deadened traditional approach among its psychiatrists . . . the deadening is epidemic among all traditional groups.

Many medical groups have what is called a journal club in which members meet regularly to discuss the medical literature and related topics. At a meeting of the psychiatric association's journal club it was announced that the following monthly discussion would be given by Dr. Barnard (a "safe" and "in" member) on group therapies, including sensitivity groups. Following an impulse, I asked the stocky, perennially cigar smoking Dr. Barnard if I could share the program with him and give a demonstration of some group sensory awareness techniques by way of introducing an experience to the members beyond just "talking about" it and he readily agreed. Safe as he is, he's also more open and flexible than most of the others.

So, at the dinner meeting the following month, with twenty or so psychiatrists seated around a long wide white tableclothed wooden table, Dr. Barnard gave a journalistically formal, factual, rather dull presentation of various group therapies. As he spoke, I looked around at the isolated, well-groomed, well-dressed, stiffly proper psychiatrists with their vague contactless, inward-looking eyes . . . almost all smoking pipes, cigarettes, cigars. How was I going to get these immobilized people moving . . . how wrench them out of the safe ensconcement of their separating armchairs? When it was my turn to talk, I said I would introduce them to some techniques used in sensitivity training and encounter groups by giving them some exercises in sensory awareness, and I invited them to leave the table and come out to the center of the room. About half of the psychiatrists stood up and joined me; the others refused to budge. I then brought up the question of whether or not we should ask the seated ones to leave, and I asked the standing group how they felt about being observed and what they would like to do about this. They decided to let the "observers" stay, even though these wouldn't be participating directly.

I then asked the participating ones to cut out the external visual stimuli by closing their eyes and then getting in touch with themselves, their feelings, how their bodies stood in space, the feel of the air space around their bodies and the surface of their bodies, how their heads were sitting on their shoulders, and whether they were leaning on one foot or standing squarely on both. I invited them to mill around and reach out to touch one another and explore one another's hands, keeping their eyes closed and remaining silent. They grimaced and seemed to behave as though I had suggested the forbidden. And then ensued a remarkable scene—these men who, in the context of that group, were the brave ones barely dared to leave the spot they were standing on . . . they reached out their hands, often unbalancing their bodies in their reaching out while their feet remained rooted. I encouraged moving and reaching and contacting in as gentle, tentative, and nonthreatening a manner as possible. Some of them, with my cajoling, did manage to move more . . . but what many of them wound up with was a position with arms stretched out sideways almost at shoulder level, holding one another's hands in a lineup with about five gingerbreadlike figures with legs and arms spread out, connected only by their outstretched hands, and with no perceptible movement despite my encouragings to explore the hands they were holding and to allow their feelings to emerge. That scene of the stiff gingerbread men has never left me—how sad! One or two sets of twos managed to allow more individual exploration. But the awkward, pained lineup of the five separated gingerbread men, unexplored and unexploring, was an overwhelming sight. In all the groups I've ever participated in, from college encounter groups, patients' groups, professional groups (these are notoriously the most uptight of all, as most group leaders know) . . . I've never, never seen such a rigid, frightened, awkward, unmoving group. Their immobility, together with the even greater granite immobility of the ones seated at the table, shed some light on the common lack of real movement toward health on the part of the average psychiatric patient, lending credence to the studies showing the lack of effectiveness of psychiatric treatment as compared to no treatment at all.

I suggested a few other things to the participating group, like milling around with their eyes open and allowing themselves to look at each other and be looked at; I asked them to allow only eye contact with no verbal interchange. Here again the sad result— the sidewise glance, the averted gaze, the embarrassed smile, the red-faced discomfiture.

However, despite all the restraints and immobilities, when we all returned to join the others at the damned hard, separating wooden white-clothed table, there was an air of unusual excitement among those who had volunteered. One by one they spontaneously offered their responses to this experience, just about all were left with good feelings, some even felt high and said so. Whereupon those in the other world of looker-on-vicarious-experiencers began "analyzing" what had just happened. One man scoffed at there being anything new here and gave an obscure, lengthy Freudian interpretation of what had happened (literally armchair therapizing); another called it hypnosis in a derogatory manner; one by one they criticized, analyzed, disparaged the entire experience, while the ones who had had the experience retained their good feelings and some even glowed throughout the rest of the meeting. It was the most alive journal club meeting I had ever attended.

But do you see what I mean about psychiatrists? No wonder they are afraid to go to parties where they might be seen by their patients! If patients could but pierce the tin-god plating and see them as they really are, what a healthy humanizing experience it could be. The psychiatrists themselves might be cured.

In that club meeting, the one thing the psychiatrists seemed to fear absolutely, in common with most uptight adults, was looking silly or foolish. To quell this fear they chose to limit their alive experiencing in order to maintain a proper decorum. So—right now—let's enter this fear—allow yourself to think of a silliness, a foolish act that you can perform in front of another person and face the risk of carrying it out. What dread consequence do you imagine? Come now, the sky didn't really fall on Chicken Little, no matter how silly she acted. Try it—chance it—risk it—humanize yourself (and save ten ridiculous years on the couch—the silliest act of all).

One day I saw Neil, a forty-five-year-old man who walked, talked, and thought like a computer. He was pleasant enough, proper, tried to be "nice" and cooperate with my prodding him into some, one, any-at-all spontaneous movement. He converted my urging into demands that he dutifully carried out in a rigidly controlled manner.

E: Can you right now let yourself fantasize a spontaneous action . . . anything at all . . . just let go and imagine something.

N: I'm blank—nothing comes to mind. I feel blocked. I guess I've never been very spontaneous.

E: Look, right now I can think of letting myself jump up and down, run around this room, swing my arms around, do a head-stand. Just let yourself free to imagine any spontaneous motion.

N: I guess the only time I'm spontaneous is when I'm having an orgasm and my body is jerking.

E: Good! Let yourself picture that.

N: (Pause.) It's not easy—I wonder if I'm even controlled when I'm having an orgasm.

E: Go to the couch and let your body move as though you're having an orgasm—just let go and let your body move.

N: (Goes to couch after looking at me incredulously; makes some comment about not being able to do this without a partner and I tell him to visualize a partner. He lies belly down on the couch, the upper part of his body supported on two rigid stalks of arms and he moves his pelvis laboriously like someone moving a ton of bricks. The tension and strain is evident throughout his body—the holding back and the control. Despite more encouragement from me to let himself move more freely, he continues to get even more rigid.)

I finally give up on that approach and stand there wondering how to get his spontaneity flowing. And then I begin to realize that I have to do something spontaneous as an example and stop talking "about" spontaneity. The silliest thing I can think of enters my mind, I hesitate a moment, and then leap over to the half-drawn drapes drawn to the side of the sliding glass doors and wrap myself in them, around and around, with just my head protruding. I feel silly, we both laugh, and Neil visibly relaxes. We then go on to explore his fear of ridicule and humiliation, which he claims as a dominant theme in his life. I think a one-week's course in audacious silliness with Jerry Rubin and the Yippies would do him more good than a half-year's therapy with me, but we're here, he and I, and we'll see how it goes.

Psychiatrity in practice in the United States is one big con job . . . and a giant put-down. Keep the patient down while the psychiatrist gets elevated beyond the human touch. Keep the psychiatrist impersonal, out of reach, unsullied by reality while the patient goes groveling among his complexes. Yes, psychiatrists are afraid to go to parties with their patients because they're more uptight about this than their patients are and they're afraid it might show. If their patients should see them acting human, flirting with other men's wives in front of their own wives, acting ill at ease socially and drinking too much, laughing at dirty jokes . . . yes, and even going to the bathroom!—it would destroy the tin-god image and decrease the worship and obeisance of the patient.

It's time this murderous myth was exploded—it's time people (patients and their psychiatrists) began to act like people with one another. It's time people knew the things about the hidden tragic elements beneath the psychiatric con game that makes the suicide statistics in this country *higher* for psychiatrists than for any other professional group (more than twice as high as for other physicians, seven times higher than for the general population—which means the psychiatrist is much more apt to kill himself than is the patient he's treating). It's time people knew such things that make the children of psychiatrists more irrevocably screwed up and damaged than any other group of kids. And this will go on and on until we breathe some human breath into the whole scene, explode the con game, destroy the tin god, save the psychiatrist from his own suicidal myth, and get everyone more real, more *animal real*.

Psychoanalysis—I have a patient who was in analysis with a reputable and highly thought of analyst for four years, three times a week . . . (count up the hours on that one!) . . . at the end of which time his hand no longer shook when he had to sign his name on business documents. He is a leaden, "nice" guy with dead-ened feelings . . . he had a conflagration burning in his mar-riage that was *never discussed* . . . not once in those four years . . . (what is reality when such an insane situation of four years' duration is subsumed under the august title of psychoanalytic treat-ment . . . and *this* is called reality, sanity, scientific validity, nor-malcy?—Jesus God, save me from such treatment).

Look, Freud was great—he developed a great tool to investigate the unconscious or whatever you want to call it. It's a fabulous *investigative* tool—but don't therapize me or my brothers and sisters with it. God dammit, you analysts, confess . . . own up to it—you have a vested interest in keeping the tool sharpened because you won't accept any other tools—you paid too high a price for yours—but own up to it—you get poor results, worse results than with any other form of psychotherapeutic approach . . . the only thing I can say in your favor is that if you're a purist about your lack of contact and noninvolvement, you usually don't prescribe medication. In this regard, and only in this, you're at least a step ahead of your psychiatric brethren who drug their patients out of contact. Come, admit it—you are a dying breed, gasping your death groans, with only a past glory to nebulously hold onto. If you admit this and can become desperate enough and frustrated enough with self-doubts, your pain will lead you to a magnificent discovery—*contact*—touching a patient's eyes with your own, touching his guts and soul with your own. Come now, don't you see how blind you make your patients when they can't look at you? Don't you *see* how blind you become when you won't look at them? Ha! you pluck out your own eyes!

68

I am reminded of an adolescent girl, a real tough egg, who entered my office reluctantly, all but forced by her parents. She spent the entire session avoiding looking straight at me and was sullen and resistant despite various attempts on my part to engage her interest. I was frustrated and disheartened. At the end of the session she got up, still sullen, and moved to the door. Suddenly, without plan, I rushed to her, grabbed her arm, which shocked her into looking at me, and blurted out: "Hey, Carla—I want to see you again. Maybe next time we can make it." Our eyes met fully, and at that moment I knew I had gotten in.

She went on, after several sessions, to befriend me and gradually to give up drugs. When she left the state to go to school she continued to write to me. Contact . . . eyes looking . . . hands reaching out!

To the uninitiated who might ask—but if the patient gets such poor results with psychoanalysis why does he stay in treatment? . . . I would like to explain how one gets hooked into staying. First of all, the lying-down position, not seeing but being seen by the person of the therapist, adds to the sense of the omnipotence of the therapist and the insignificance of the patient . . . (if you don't get this or don't believe it, put yourself in a room with a reclining person and look at him while he can't see you—then, reverse roles—see what I mean?). Then, too, the patient is encouraged to dwell on early memories and relationships and transfers much to the nonperson of the analyst—this entire process is regressive, encouraging a kind of psychic dependency. (Imagine— my house burning for four years . . . yes, my wife going depressed and crazy . . . and myself going dead . . . and after four years of treatment all I got to show for it is the steadiness of my hand. Man! If that isn't a master con job, a tied-down dependency to which I— the patient—offer no tiny note in protest . . . no, on the contrary, I think what a great job the doctor did in steadying my hand.)

Wake up! Save yourselves! Save me from ecclesiastic rigidity under whatever flag it goes!

The fantastically infantile struggles that were waged in New York while I was there, like—oh no, if it's not five days a week then it's not *analysis* . . . according to Holy Scripture, analysis is defined and limited to five visits a week . . . anything less is not, by definition, called analysis. Imagine that upstart, Sandor Rado, starting his own school at Columbia University and calling it analysis even though it's only *four* days a week! Why, it's not the real thing, and we won't consider anyone as being truly analyzed if they go to that school. The only true school and the only true practitioners are the New York Psychoanalytic Institute and their analysts. And even worse heretics are the Horneyites . . . imagine calling themselves analysts and they see patients only three times a week . . . we don't even recognize them, of course. . . . (Shades of how many angels dance on the head of a pin . . . and other such medievalisms.) Wow! Such crap! And not a word of this is exaggerated—it used to be a major topic of conversation, debate, and fury among psychiatrists. Can you really take these infants as men of science? Would you put your maturity and your strengths into their immature, weak hands? And heaven forbid if anyone comes along with any real innovation beyond the number of angels . . . visits per week . . . dancing . . . hey, Talmudists are OK, but please leave them in the Middle Ages with their biblical pursuits and not in the middle of your guts. Please, don't put your burning-down marriages, your kids, your houses in their unseen and probably nonexistent hands. Find someone who has hands reaching out to your hands, who is not afraid to cry for your tears . . . (and his own) . . . bleed for your wounds . . . (and his own) . . . laugh for your joys . . . (and his own). Don't go to a dead man who practices dead arts to help you live and love. If you would only open your ears to these infantilisms and petty bickerings, I'm sure you would stay away from such people—for people who have their *heads* filled with such nonsense allow little room in their *hearts* for the real concerns with the blood and guts matters that drive most of us into therapy.

Intact, aloof, separate! In my psychiatric residency it was common knowledge to all the residents that the New York Psycho-analytic Institute always picked as candidates for their school the most rigid, isolated, and disturbed personalities among us for admission. Digest that one for a while, and let us leave the analysts sitting in their sterile offices and go on to an encounter with the Master Group at a New York Psychoanalytic Institute meeting almost two decades ago. On this occasion, the institute members allegedly met to discuss Reich's masterpiece, *Character Analysis.* Actually, they met to crucify Wilhelm Reich. (In character analytic work as described in his book, Reich expounds on his theories of muscular armoring as related to emotional and character disturbances . . . for example, a rigid-tight-stiff character literally has stiff neck musculature . . . I might add, also, a tight asshole, constipation being a frequent concomitant of this type of disturbance. I'll discuss more of Reich's work later.) The title of the meeting was "Character Analysis," and they imported an analyst from Chicago to present the major discussion. I was quite naïve in those days and was therefore astonished at the venomous and bitter tone of the talk coming from a respected psychoanalyst. Then, one by one . . . as I sat in amazement . . . I heard members of the Psychoanalytic Institute get up on the podium and hurl infantile but nonetheless abrasive invective at Reich. The senior member of the group (a mild-looking white-haired man) actually yelled excitedly: "Everything Reich said that was good came from Freud . . . everything bad came from Reich!" Finally, the last speaker, the only young fellow on the program, started his comments with an apology . . . literally, a real apology! . . . which he directed to the senior members . . . apologizing for having something positive to say about Reich. After some complimentary remarks about the value of Reich's contributions (spoken in a meek, apologetic tone of voice), he went on to vilify Reich in much the same manner as had the others.

Seekers of the truth? These are the infants to whom you attribute such Father-Godlike qualities and on whose couches you lie wasting your guts.

And Reich's crime? He went beyond the Victorianism of an abstract id concept into the somatic realities of the function of an orgasm.

And Reich's other crime? The crime I'm committing now—club members are supposed to be loyal to The Club, no matter what. Wilhelm Reich suffered the fate of most innovators, of most people who broke through the blind spots of traditional faiths into a vision of the future. In his early professional days Reich was already translating into concrete physical terms the psychoanalytic libido theories of Freud. He started sex clinics in Germany where he dealt with the sexual miseries and the manifold consequences of sexual malfunctioning in his patients—dealt openly with a subject, sex, which was most often closed and covered. In his work with sexual repressions and orgastic disturbances, he carried Freud's libido theory to its practical and extreme conclusion, believing the functioning of the total personality to be directly correlated with the level of orgastic response. Later, in this country, his focus on the physical aspects of sex involved him in physical and physiological research that led to his discovery of what he termed "orgone," or life energy, an energy that he believed to be omnipresent. According to Reich, in neurotic individuals the free flow of this energy is dammed up, incarcerated in rigid musculature in various parts of the body—the rigid defensive muscles he termed "armor"—and there is a resultant disturbance in the full orgastic release in these individuals. In his therapeutic work with patients he directly attacked the rigid musculature or armoring, be it the jaw, neck, or other body part, and he found that the physical approach to the armor helped the patient to break through into allowing a free flow of energy throughout the body. Because he believed his orgone energy existed not only in animals but in the atmosphere as well, he developed a means of accumulating this energy in a box whose walls were composed of layers of certain materials such as aluminum and steel. He felt this led to a greater concentration of the orgone energy within the box. Whether patients received benefit from sitting in the box as a placebo effect or otherwise I am not prepared to evaluate. I always had my own doubts about it and never used it in my practice. However, when the FDA's attack on Reich was at its height there were wild stories circulated about the "sex box" and the "orgasm box," stories that became more fanciful and more elaborately lewd as time went on. Reich was jailed on the grounds of selling the Orgone Accumulator across state lines. (I want to add here that the orgone therapists whom I knew were men of integrity who sincerely believed in the efficacy of the Orgone Accumulator.) He ultimately refused to accept legal counsel and felt that no jury of lay people was equipped to evaluate the scientific validity of his work. He claimed that the FDA never carried out the experiments on the Accumulator as he had outlined in his book. The psychoanalysts accused Reich of being paranoid. The FDA, on a rampage, ordered almost all of Reich's books burned. Reich ultimately died while in jail, respected and admired by his co-workers and followers, denigrated and vilified by most of his psychoanalytic colleagues and the FDA.

The use of the psychiatrist to carry out the interests not of the patient but of the established order (often in contradiction to the patient's interests) has been studied and validated by Dr. Thomas Szasz, a brilliant psychoanalyst. My own father had a personal experience with one such establishment psychiatrist, whom I shall call Dr. Weiman.

When my Dad, who came to Philadelphia from Kiev in 1914 at the age of seventeen, was getting his discharge (honorable) from the United States Army (Yeah!—he actually enlisted . . . I think partly to get away from his older brother's domination and partly because bread was hard to come by in those days, especially for a Russian Jew . . . I wonder what was harder—the bread in 1917 or the battlegrounds he had to fight on in France with the subsequent nightmares of bombs and blood?) . . . well, when he got out of the army he applied for rehabilitation assistance (paperhanging was a starving trade in those days), and before offering this, the government sent him for medical clearance, which included a psychiatric exam. It was determined that he qualified for schooling as

73

an auto mechanic and he was sent to Spring Garden Institute. After more than one year my father had to be reevaluated for extension of his schooling, and he was sent to Dr. Weiman. During my father's interview with him, he was trying to knock down my father's school extension. According to my father, "he started asking me different questions about my family, like . . . do I come from a big family. I told him there were nine children . . . and then he asked me if anyone was nuts in the family . . . and I told him no. Then he says . . . you're Jewish, aren't you? . . . and I says yeah . . . then he says it's damn funny in a big family like that there shouldn't be at least one nut . . . so I told him—look, Doctor, you're Jewish too, aren't you? . . . and he told me that was different, that he comes from a family where there's all doctors and lawyers and things like that . . . so I says—how do you know my family— whether we have doctors and lawyers in my family?" My father concluded: "He just said it to make himself feel big against me." And—the school extension was denied. *But*—justice had another way of ruling . . . right after my father left the office: "There was this guy who was really shell-shocked who walked in to get examined for government assistance . . . and after two minutes Weiman ran out with a black eye. I asked the guy what had happened and he said Weiman asked him whether his mother and father were crazy and things like that, so he hauled off and hit him . . . Weiman was trying to get everyone's disturbance traced to heredity so the government wouldn't have to shell out any dough." Here was clearly the psychiatrist in the role of the establishment's pawn.

My own early contact with psychiatrists occurred during my first year at medical school when, still in bobby socks and pigtails, I attended whatever psychiatric meetings I could, including those of the solemn Philadelphia Psychiatric Society. At these, I always offered my own views, undaunted by the black suits and ties of the formal senior members of the society.

At a meeting of the Citron Psychiatric Hospital, a resident presented a patient to the staff, and his conclusions seemed to me to be far off the beam, having missed an important aspect of the patient's psychodynamics, I thought. So, I got up and supplied the missing insights . . . wearing my six-dollar nondescript, ill-fitting wool suit, my brown flat-heeled oxfords, and ever-present bobby socks (with or without holes?). Later that evening the head of the hospital approached me, obviously impressed, and offered me a residency at his hospital and an offer to help get me any Philadelphia internship I desired. He seemed amazed that I was only a freshman medical student. But I didn't accept his offer . . . even then I was eager to get to New York and also to get as far away as possible from my southern-women-dominated medical college.

My next significant contact with psychiatrists, after the long years of medical school and internship, occurred in my psychiatric residency when I finally reached my glory—pure psychiatry—no blood vessels and nerves to trace, no skeletal structures to memorize, no distractions—just the real stuff—real work with real patients, the whole person, not just a toenail, kidney, or liver. I had arrived!

My residency experience at a Veterans Administration Hospital in New York was magnificent. The chief of the neuropsychiatric service was unusual. For the first time in my professional schools and training, I met an administrator who not only allowed but seemed to admire my uniqueness. When I first met him for the job interview, I arrived bright-eyed, eager, with a volume of Freud under my arm. He was obviously taken with me and hired me on the spot. He was beautiful to me . . . gave me free reign with my patients and never did anything to squelch my enthusiasm and ardor. I was able to give my patients as much attention and contact as I wished, and had the thrill of seeing them get well. At no time did I give any patient shock treatment or any medication . . . just personal contact, human contact.

One of my first patients on the closed wards was a young black man who thought he was General MacArthur and that his skin was all different colors like a rainbow. He saw cats coming out of the television set and was in a constant state of panic. He had developed a persecution complex on his job and thought his boss was out to kill him. Right then and there, at that very first interview, I decided to devote myself to him in the hope of curing him. Almost all the other residents would have immediately sent him to the shock ward (as though shock can substitute for the real need for contact). I saw him every single day; I got to see his father who was a severe, demanding man from the British West Indies. As soon as my patient began to trust me, I talked about his resentments toward his father's strict authority. Day by day the hallucinations and delusions melted one by one, his panic state subsided, and he became more or less normal in behavior. At this point we touched on his relationship with his boss upon whom the patient seemed to have displaced much of the buried resentment he had had toward his father. He began to see his paranoid ideas about his boss as a projection of his repressed feelings toward his father, the formula being something like this: My father is cruel to me . . . I hate my father . . . my boss is a father figure . . . I project my hate of my father onto my boss . . . I begin to think my boss hates me . . . he will do me harm . . . he's out to get me . . . help, I must run away!

In about a month after admission I transferred this patient to the open wards and continued to see him. I met his wife and saw his father several times. With the insights the patient had gained and his contact with his strengths he was able to stand up for himself in front of his father and then to leave the hospital after a couple of months and go back to his job and face his boss. I later heard from him . . . he was doing well, his wife had given birth to another baby, and he weathered this and other storms very well. I'm convinced that shock treatment would never have achieved this result for this man . . . on the contrary, it might have prevented it.

When that patient had shown such marked improvement, the senior resident approached me and suggested I present him at a case conference. I agreed. Then the resident said that he'd like to give the patient an amytal interview to get the "underlying dynamics" so he could present a fuller picture in his discussion of my presentation. I didn't like the idea, but he assured me he had given many of these and they were harmless. I was naïve, unknowledgeable, just a few months into my residency, and I consented. During the amytal interview, the patient began to express his fears. Nothing new was discovered. After the amytal, the patient began developing his hallucinations and his paranoid ideas again and he became even more fearful. It took many, many hours of being with him to get him back the gains he had lost through the amytal experience. The wounds healed more slowly the second time around.

Over the ensuing years of my practice, I have developed a healthy paranoid distrust of drugs, even "harmless" ones, and drug dispensers, and I shall remain forever distrustful. What the senior resident was doing was to run a procedure on the patient *for his own curiosity* and to make a more brilliant case discussion for his own *ego*. How many doctors at this very moment are thus motivated? This is an abuse; a patient comes to a doctor for treatment, for help—if the doctor *uses* the patient for any purpose other than that which the patient pays for and contracts for, it is the deepest breach of human contract, a violation and assault on human trust. (How many of those thousands of surgical and medical patients were told they were being used as guinea pigs for the thalidomide experiment in this country?)

Let's now look at a couple of psychiatric "experts" at close range. I recall a child psychiatrist at a Board of Education guidance clinic where I worked for some years. With every patient this child psychiatrist presented at the staff conferences, without exception, his solution was to remove the child from his parents . . . it was so ludicrous as to be almost a laughing matter among the staff that he was so predictable in his recommendation to send the kids away from their homes. (What does this say about his feelings—or lack of them—toward his own kids?)

And still another expert comes to mind—this time a neuropsychiatrist with a grand reputation in New York as well as the rest of the country, an expert in child psychiatry, an author of several important works, widely accepted in the psychiatric community, innovator of many tests for childhood schizophrenia, organizer of several psychiatric and neurological research projects. Early in my practice, I worked in a child psychiatric clinic he had set up in one

77

of the New York City hospitals. He saw a five-year-old girl one time in a diagnostic interview and recommended that she be sent to a mental institution. The mother was greatly distressed at this suggestion and objected, and I saw the girl and her mother in a psychiatric consultation. What I saw was a frightened, bewildered mother and a pretty, red-haired little girl who was immature for her age and suffered from some phobic reactions. I took my job in my hands, told the mother that I disagreed with the recommendation of the clinical director, and that, in fact, I was optimistic about the prognosis. I began to see the little girl weekly and occasionally saw the mother and child together. The mother was primarily seen weekly by the psychiatric social worker. In those days they and I still used the archaic, wasteful, nonsensical approach of separating the treatment of different family members . . . many rigid clinics and treatment centers with some of the highest reputations are *still* using this preposterous approach—in fact, the majority of psychiatrists and psychoanalysts do likewise, reacting to the thought of seeing another family member with the horror with which one withdraws from a leper. This is the penalty one pays for replacing common human sense with mechanical dogma, resulting in interminable therapy and despair.

I'm reminded of a thirty-eight-year-old divorcée who complained that she was unable to talk to her sixteen-year-old son, that he wouldn't listen to her, that she sacrificed so much for him and he was so ungrateful and never showed any appreciation, and on and on. Having been long liberated from the wasteful separatist approach to problems in a family (thanks to humanizing influences of people like Virginia Satir), I invited her to bring her son to the next session.

When they arrived, I asked them to sit face to face, look at each other, and discuss their problems. The skinny, pale-faced teen-ager was tense, defensive, guarded, closemouthed. The mother was accusatory, complaining, whining, and, above all, wide openmouthed. The picture they presented in just those first few moments was worth an encyclopedia of words and a year of "therapeutic investigations." Most striking was the absolute avoidance between these two of any eye contact. The mother's eyes, although her face was fronting her son's, were off to the side in an upward direction, and she appeared to be delivering her tale of woe to the air. The son's eyes were held in a downward gaze as if finding some interest in the patterns on the rug.

I did very little in that session except to interrupt the scene once the foregoing picture was fully revealed and to tell them I had asked them to look at each other, which neither one was doing. They both looked guiltily shamefaced and, for the first time in that session, their eyes met in a common awareness of guilt. It was their first moment's direct contact, and a communicating smile brushed across their faces simultaneously. I then asked them to stay looking at each other and express what they were feeling toward the other at that moment. Silence—the eyes went off, returned, went off again. Embarrassment. Awkwardness. Avoidance. Tension mounting. "I know it's hard for people in the same family to look at one another . . . just do the best you can and don't talk unless you have a feeling to put into words," I said softly.

The atmosphere was charged; the awkward self-conscious smiles were changing to looks of solemnity and seriousness; tears came to the mother's eyes as she looked fully into her son's eyes. She said: "I love you." The boy was obviously touched, his voice came out falteringly: "I love you too, Mom." They both had tears in their eyes by now—I asked them to do whatever they felt like doing, and, after some hesitation, the mother got up and embraced her son with both crying more openly by now.

After this, I suggested they go on right now to make their demands openly on each other and see if they can agree on some mutually acceptable contract for living together. The mother made a list of specific requests, the son made his, and they finally found some measure of mutually acceptable compromise and agreement.

That was the entire session—less than an hour's worth. In her session the next week the mother said she couldn't get over the "miracle" that happened. "Barry is a new person—he's never been so cooperative—he even offers to run errands for me before I ask him to." Several months later, the mother said her communication with her son was continuing to grow and deepen. It seemed they had finally crossed over a bridge and never again would go back to their land of separation and misery.

My guess is that therapies that at base look to separate people and separately "analyze" the reasons for gaps in communication never or rarely see any constructive bridging of those gaps. But real therapy is connected with pain, is scary and rough and oh, so ridiculously simple.

Getting back now to that little red-haired girl; one-half year after treatment was started, she was in school, walking up and down the stairs she had earlier dreaded, and showing good functioning with her peers and siblings and in her school adjustment. After one year she was discharged, and a year afterward her mother wrote me telling me of her continued progress.

I'll never forget the misery and the tormented look on the mother's face when she first told me that the expert on childhood schizophrenia, Dr. Martin, had recommended a mental institution for her daughter and how the look melted when I, just a couple of years out of my residency . . . a mere upstart . . . told her I didn't at all agree, in fact, I felt it was contraindicated, and that I believed her daughter could be helped considerably more by living at home.

Incidentally, Dr. Martin himself suffered from a severe telephone phobia—on the limited instances when he spoke on the phone he was overwhelmed with anxieties. Yes, trust the crazy experts too much and you or your kids will wind up in the booby hatch.

And now let's move in to get an even closer look into the psychiatrist's head. But first, please say this word: "Engagement." Now vary it as follows and repeat a few times: "Engage, engaging, engagement." How alive! Repeat the phrase a few more times and get in touch with your feelings while saying it. And now, say: "Diagnosis"—say it a few times and then repeat the following: "Diagnose,

diagnosing, diagnosis." How dead and deadening. Psychiatric diagnosing is as deadening a process as psychoanalysis except that it
doesn't last as long.

Now, what happens while I, as psychiatrist, sit here trying to
diagnose you? I am disengaged not only from you but from my own
feelings. I go through the labyrinth of textbook learnings and didactic instructions trying to find the correct pigeonhole in which to
place the myriad symptoms and stances you present to me. In this
process, even my own processes, which have been so highly trained
and educated and coerced into pigeonhole thinking, become confused . . . (because how can you be a human being and still fit
into a pigeonhole? . . . hard enough to fit pigeons into them and
have them stay there . . . ask any physical anthropologist). Yeah,
you got it . . . it just can't be done . . . not to a human being.
As soon as things seem to fit, a whole bunch of other things jump
out and contradict it.

Try it out this way—astrology describes twelve major pigeon-
holes. If you want very much to believe in the stars in this way, you
see only the things about you that fit into your particular astrological
pigeonhole and then, of course, you're a believer . . . and then
maybe even a proselytizer. OK, what about all the things about you
that you keep out of your sight in order to have a perfect fit? (Just
the way psychiatrists do in diagnosing a patient.) Now, try an experiment—take yourself a different sign for a moment and pretend it's
yours. Then read it, trying to fit into it, and keep out all parts of
your description that don't fit. Chances are you'll find some way to
get another perfect fit (just the way psychiatrists do . . . there's
always a way to get a perfect fit). All you need is a combination of
faith and denial to do it—psychiatrists have both . . . faith in
what their books say, in what their teachers have handed down,
and denial of what their innards are revealing about the patient and
what the patient's innards are uniquely, unpigeonholily revealing
about themselves.

As for the astrological believers, more and more since Hair's Age
of Aquarius has caught on, I have the following experience:

A.B. (Astrological Believer): What sign are you under?

A.M. (Agnostic Me): Scorpio.

A.B. (gleefully): *Right on! Out of sight!*

A.M. (naïvely, really wanting to hear): Why, tell me, what's special about Scorpio?

A.B.: Well, uhh, I don't really know. I'm not really into it *that* much.

I like to hear that I'm under an out-of-sight sign, and I know that particular kind of astrological believer would say: "Out of sight" no matter what sign I said. Still, somehow it's better than "pleased to meet you" . . . it really does make me feel special when they say it that way to me and I get a warm glow toward them—special.

So much for pigeonholing diagnoses that may make the psychiatrist feel better but benefit the patient not an iota. As for engagement, when your car's gears are not engaged, your car won't run. When your therapist and you are not engaged, your therapy won't run. The trouble with most people in psychotherapeutic treatment (analysis, as I've said, is not treatment, it is dissection which has its place as an investigative or research tool but not as therapy) is that they have been so long in a disengaged standstill, they don't know what real movement feels like. In fact, this is part of that underlying conspiracy between doctor and patient I've been talking about that keeps patients immobilized in treatment for years—"You don't move too much to threaten our comfortable, safe standstill and neither will I"—they say to each other while the years tick on and the blood is raped. Do you want to test out this thesis and take some risk in engaging? The next time you (therapist or therapee) go to the office where therapy is supposed to be happening, do something totally out of the routine . . . engage the other person's eyes with conscious intent to do so and feel what comes out of those eyes and feel what's coming out of your own. There's a direct beeline between your eyes and your belly. Feel what's in your belly; feel what's coming out of his belly. Chances are, when you do this, you'll find *nothing* coming out. If you must use words, you might try something like: "It's time for a change." The result will probably still be *nothing,* but as you continue to open your eyes to the eyes of your beholder (if he dares look back), there may emerge from either or both of you some slight evidence of discomfort, awkwardness, embarrassment. Good!—something is stirring . . . and once there's even a breath of movement, you both have a chance for real change. It's the stillness, the safety, and the comfort that violate the natural flow of life toward its climax. And the real work of therapy is to reestablish this flow.

Now, if the other person withdraws from your reach (like by prescribing/asking for pills, stopping treatment, calling for a straitjacket), again good! At least you stop the *folie à deux* and you're moving somewhere toward constructive change . . . and you both learn what almost no analytic patient has learned from his analyst-playing God: no one person is indispensable utterly in another person's life—crutches are replaceable, even mother's milk can be gotten from other mothers. And when you destroy the myth of indispensability, you may move on to find a real person to work with, to move with. And . . . you won't get into the fairly common morass that a woman psychiatric resident I knew got into when she followed her analyst to Europe, irrationally believing he was utterly necessary to her life. He was a senior member of the New York Psychoanalytic Institute, and I suppose he suffered from a similar delusion for he did nothing to discourage her from running after him! By the way, some years later, after her return to America, she learned that the "psychogenic headaches" that her analyst had been analyzing and labeling with fancy, accusatory psychodynamic formulations turned out to be a brain tumor. George Gershwin, you were sadly not to be the only victim of psychoanalysis of a brain tumor. Well, fortunately the adoration of the analyst and the "my analyst says" craze are diminishing as reality bombards them. But there are still too many analysts and patients clutching at the *comfort* in their relationship as though it were a lifeline.

Only when we leave the persons of our parents and their substitutes outside of ourselves can we really begin to grow-flow into our own person. What is so terrible about this growth that people clutch on to an ersatz lifeline, routinizing and disengaging and deadening their innards? *What a terrible price to pay for safety and comfort!*

Contact—use your guts, man. What does your belly tell you about that cold, unfeeling, probably sleeping person sitting immobile hour after hour . . . what do you think happens to *him* after spending most of his work-life in this depersonalized immobility?

Hey, there's a great thing Fritz Perls says, a beautiful insight into Freud's couch technique. He says that Freud was phobic and couldn't stand to have people looking at him . . . and his phobia became the cornerstone (I might add, the gravestone) of psychoanalysis, the raison d'être of the horizontal patient and the vertical analyst. Now, Fritz Perls—there's a great innovator for me—he contributed to a complete change in my encountering patients, in my becoming more a human being in relation to the human being there before me. I had read similar concepts in Harry Stack Sullivan (also in Fromm and Horney) years before I discovered Perls, but they remained concepts . . . with Perls I had a breakthrough toward humanizing my whole contact with patients, with others, and with myself.

Speaking of phobic separation, imagine the separation between doctor and patient around those large office desks! I even had one myself early in my practice when I was insecure enough to want to keep some distance—wow! In those days if I had wanted to reach out a hand to a patient I would have had to throw my shoulder out of joint reaching across all that expanse of beautifully grained walnut. Now I see patients in my living room—face to face—with only a little air space between us . . . and when I move closer to hold their hands we're almost knee to knee.

My farewell epilogue to psychiatrists and psychoanalysts gives me a chance to introduce the idea of how our behavior affects us . . . how we become what we do . . . how we turn into the person we behave like. My epilogue to the Dead Men practicing their deadly ensconcing arts in a vignette from my play, *The Drugstore,* which takes place for the most part in a literal drugstore (for are we not living symbolically in a massive drugstore?).

84

THE SCENE: a Molly Goldberg type of character (Fanny) who works in the drugstore is giving a spiel to George, a black street cleaner, both of whom consider themselves as "feet people," both are energetic, taking their jobs seriously.

FANNY: . . . and do you know what part my boss uses most?

GEORGE: Well, you said he was a doctor, so it must be his hands?

FANNY: No, his "tochis" (smacking her amply protruding rear end) . . . he's a psychiatrist . . . he *sits* all day.

GEORGE (getting "respectful" again): Well, then, what I said about his being lazy and a thief just don't apply.

FANNY: Why not? Look, not wishing to say anything unkind, but after sitting hour after hour, day after day, year after year . . . even if a person wasn't lazy to begin with, how long do you think it would take before he *did* get lazy? And—it's not thievery to take money for just sitting? And do you know what else I hear? Sometimes when the patient isn't looking . . . you know, when they're lying down on the couch, some psychiatrists even *fall asleep!* I wouldn't want to mention any names, of course . . . but . . .

Yes, not wishing to say anything unkind, I feel like Hamlet tormentedly saying to his mother: "I must be cruel only to be kind." If my angry slashing of psychiatrists and psychoanalysts will save even one person somewhere from being further dehumanized by the dead men with their deadly arts or resuscitate one deadly practitioner enough for him to take a real look at himself and his patient, then my assault will have been kind, indeed.

4

MEDICAL SADISM:
SHOCK AND ELECTRICITY
ICE PICK AND LOBOTOMY

Let's now look at a not so constructive type of slashing—assault on people called "mental patients." Once upon a time psychiatrically ill people were cared for in their own homes, adjusted to by the community. Some even had special powers attributed to them and were looked up to and treated with respect. Then more civilized cultures emerged and the mentally ill were locked up. During one era they were beaten to drive out the evil spirits. At another time they were put in chains. In twentieth-century America they were locked in back wards of institutions and allowed to sit, naked, in puddles of feces. Despite a few bright lights along the way, like Pinel who freed them from their chains and Freud who tried to understand them, their gloomy fate worsened with the advent of the modern medicine man and his bag of awesome technological gimmicks.

Although medical sadism takes many forms, like womb and breast ripping, probably the most vicious, and the one over which outraged Nature sheds her most agonizing tears, is the brain cell killing by psychiatrists and neurosurgeons with their ECT—electroconvulsive treatment, commonly known as electroshock treatment (hey, there's that "treatment" stuff again!)—and their lobotomies. The eighteenth-century beatings and the nineteenth-century chains were degrading, but brain cells did not die under their assault. Today, any pathologist will tell you of the death, the irreversible death, of brain cells following shock treatment. Brain cells, unlike epidermal and other tissue cells, are irreplaceable—once they're dead, they're dead forever.

Why do we put up with this sadistic onslaught? How do the medical sadists get away with it? To seek the answer, I'm brought back to the doctor theme again (the horror subsumed under that title! . . . I can't seem to let go of it until I get all the horror stuff in me flowing out from my pen to your awareness so you can beware, be wary, and dare to question . . . yes, dare even to object!).

They get away with it and we put up with it because of something basic in our relationship with all authority. It goes like this: first we put our blinders on about our parents as persons, as sexual people, and of course our parents help us do this . . . after this blinding and hypocrisizing process it doesn't take many steps to blind ourselves to what all the other authorities are doing behind their closed doors or even out in the open. Think of the idealism with which, as children, we viewed our parents and our teachers; the impossibility of thinking of them as persons like ourselves with pettinesses, petulant angers, selfish motives, frightened vulnerabilities. And most of all, the utter incredulousness attached to the idea that they are sexual persons . . . that they actually screw! Now—even now—adult as you are, with whatever sexual experience, real or fantasized, you have had, see what happens when you try to pierce the veil surrounding your parents' animality, their sexuality. (Until you do this you will, in denying them their personness, deny your own, and subject yourself to living in a should-would-unreal world.) Can you, in your mind's eye, see them nude, much less embracing, and much more less engaged in the ultimate complete embrace to say nothing of its variations! In fact, a sexual relationship between parents is so taboo from the child's point of view, it seems almost like incest.

With what a shudder do we turn from this view—from this viewing. Even those of grandparent age have not achieved this touch of reality in viewing their own parents. And this whole business . . . this cloud of secrecy . . . has been institutionalized by the Catholic Church, which condones sex for procreative purposes only. Yes, that much we can allow—sex for duty . . . to honor the procreative will of God . . . the perpetuation of the species. It's changing now, what with the establishment's getting worried about population growth. Shit!—how our myths are formed to satisfy the needs of the immediate established orders, and we poor suckers go swallowing them in, hook, line, and sinker—and how we sink beneath the myths we swallow!

And parents perpetuate the "duty" myth when they tell their children of "planting the seed" (farmers planting vegetables, producing vegetables)—the fertilization of the egg—and breathe not one breath of a whisper about *pleasure!* . . . about passion!

Yes—once we can stifle the existence of passion around and in us, an essential process in becoming a vegetable, it's an easy step to walk into the waiting murdering hands of the shockiatrists. As for the lobotomizers (talk about playing God!—this is the epitome, when a flick of the wrist creates a vegetable and uncreates a man)—when we have already given our brains and passions away in the service of becoming vegetables, the lobotomizer merely finishes the job neatly and surgically—he is our creation—we aid him in uncreating ourselves.

All psychiatrists are indoctrinated with brain-killing shock as an accepted form of "treatment," while they call themselves *doctors* . . . but who will doctor their patients' brain cells, killed forever by these brain cell murderers? What's the penalty for this crime? If not in our era, in the future, men of medicine will look with as much horror on our lobotomies, our insulin, electric, and other forms of shock-the-brain processes as we look upon the past chains of the asylum inmates. Yes, I, too, declaim with Wordsworth: "Great God, I'd rather be a pagan suckled in a creed outworn . . ." We are steeped in the muck of "civilized" bloodbaths.

During my psychiatric residency I was required to spend three months on the closed shock wards of the hospital.

I tried all my ingenuity and pleading to get out of serving my necessary time on the shock wards, but it was a mandatory service, an unbreakable rule. I knew, however, deep in my innards, that I would never push the button to run electricity through some poor guy's brain, an electrical death-to-the-gray-cells-jag that some half-assed, snot-nosed resident had blithely written down as "medical orders" after spending a pressured, hurried minimum time with the victim-patient. The orders for insulin or electric shock came from residents on the closed ward on which I had just served. Let any patient show any hyperactivity, depression, paranoia, hallucinations, and they were hastily transferred to the shock wards by the majority of the residents.

Lord! —What could I do, what with my feelings that I should not, could not, *would not* push those buttons and damage and destroy an already tormented soul? Out of the depths of my desperation, mustering whatever intelligence and cleverness I could, I hit on a research project. I presented it the same day to the chief of the neuropsychiatric service and . . . he agreed! My time on the shock wards was to be spent on my own project . . . I would not have to electrocute a single person! Hurray! Success!

My research project arose out of an encounter I had with a patient coming out of insulin coma "treatment"—he said he felt as though he had died and was walking or floating in heaven. This patient was actually, literally, close to death—he had gone down to a stage three coma—a little deeper and he would have died. I speculated that his "death experience" was actually a psychological representation of what, physiologically, was going on at that moment in his body. I set about to prove or disprove this thesis. Actually, I disproved it— patients who were close to physiological death had a lesser number of death experiences than patients who had light comas—but I got away without pushing a single electrical button, probably the only resident to thus succeed in the history of that hospital. And, to top it all, with my chief's encouragement, I wrote up the project and got it published in the American Psychiatric Association's Journal under the title "The Death Experience in Insulin Coma Treatment."

In telling this story I am reminded of a story I read a long time ago by Langston Hughes, who worked as a delivery "boy" carrying packages up and down the elevator. Whenever a white man entered the elevator, every black man was supposed to tip his hat and show respect. Hughes devised a way of not doing this and yet not facing the dire consequences to a black man in the South who dared defy this protocol. He developed a technique of suddenly busying himself with the package he'd be holding, encumbering both of his hands so that it was physically impossible for him to tip his hat. So, holding onto his packages, he held onto his dignity and subtly overcame the white man's hierarchy. In a similar way, by busying myself with my project and also by conducting group therapy sessions on the shock wards, I avoided taking part in the indignity and inhumanity of an outrageous assault on the human brain of those human patients. I maintained their humanity and my own.

About shockiatrists: I actually knew a New York City psychiatrist who opened a psychiatric clinic in Brooklyn—the rooms were tiny, unwindowed cells—and he paid residents a low fee and charged patients a relatively high fee for "treatment" . . . and there was an awful lot of shock happening at over fifty bucks a click with the profits going to this suave, elite guy who owned the clinic.

One of the commonest excuses for giving shock treatment is the diagnosis, "Depressive Reaction." The depressed patient with his self-accusatory wail frustrates the traditional psychiatrist, for the more you listen to the depressive complaints of the patient, the more you encourage the depression.

Let's look at depression for a few moments. I'll simplify the dynamics and start with the masking smile. It's a baaad anger that hides beneath a smile . . . if it gets baaaad enough, the anger, the smile turns into tears, into depression. Depressed people are angry—

every two-bit psychiatrist knows that. So what the civilized doctors have developed is a fantastic punishing device—killing brain cells—that'll teach them to be angry again!

It'll teach them, all right, but it won't cure them. The best cure for the depressed person is for him to beat up on someone else. But the psychiatrist somehow notes the anger vibes beneath the depression of his patient, responds with his own anger vibes (which he, too, keeps hidden), coupled with his frustration at not being able to reach the patient with his traditional tuned-out listening device, and then goes on a shock rampage to get *himself* out of the impasse.

With depressed patients, instead of beating their brains out, I get them to beat up my couch (the legitimate use of the couch) and beat up the air waves in my office with their furious outbursts, hidden beneath the depression, once I can get the anger flowing . . . and man, does it flow!

An internist referred Penny, a twenty-three-year-old woman, for treatment because he was afraid she would commit suicide. He thought I might have to hospitalize her and give her shock treatment, he said. He had dosed her up to the maximum with one drug after another in his attempts to "treat" her depression and told me that all drugs had so far failed to bring her out of it.

Penny was a depressed walking drugstore when she entered my office, barely dragging her body along, and contrasting remarkably with her energetic, piss-and-vinegar young husband who brought her. We established that I would see her every single day for that week and for the week following if necessary. She was very meek, agreed to everything I said, evidenced no push-back, her shoulders were bowed, she walked and talked very very slowly and with seeming effort, her face was drained of all color—corpselike. It was clear that her character attitude beneath the obvious depression was one of extreme passivity—the aggression was buried deep within. She was one of those "nice-sweet" people who always aimed to please. She talked so softly that it was hard to hear her in that first session. I explained a little about depression in general and asked her if she was resentful or angry at anyone—all she could express was how good her husband was to her, how guilty she felt at all the trouble she was causing him, how much he had to pay for all the doctor bills and staying out of work and losing pay because of her.

I told her she'd have to stop all medication—that we would work through the depression on our own without drugs and that I needed her help. At this point she felt so miserable, plus her underlying passivity, that she agreed to everything. We talked about her family situation, her husband and his temper outbursts (which she mentioned with no outward tinge of resentment), her rejecting, hard-to-get-along-with mother, and her cold, aloof father. I then invited her to pound my couch as hard as she could and let her voice connect with the action. She stood before the couch and at the most brought her hands down in a light pat—she could barely move. I told her I'd help her and that it sounded to me as though there was a lot for her to be resentful about. I took her hands in mine, raised them over her head, and brought them down forcibly to strike the couch. She gave neither resistance nor energy to the feat—she was a rag doll with no movement of her own. I asked her to yell—just to make any sound above the defeated given-up voice she was using and she let out little more than a whisper. I got more energetic myself and yelled: "I can't hear you—make it *louder!*" I got a little rise out of her with my yell, the first sign of life (psychiatrists aren't supposed to yell?). As her voice became somewhat more forceful, I yelled even louder for her to make it louder. By the end of the first session she was striking the couch, though weakly, on her own initiative. She left the office a little more hopeful than when she entered and with her shoulders less drooped.

By the third visit she was not only striking the couch but yelling almost uncontrollably. Out of her poured some fierce invectives that took me by surprise in their ferocity—Damn you! . . . Fuck you! . . . You goddamn bitch! . . . Son-of-a-bitch! . . . over and over again, bursting into heaving and sobbing when her energy was spent. The nice-sweet-good girl had become a ferocious hellion hurling out her venom. By around the beginning of the second week she suddenly arrived with makeup on, her hair done up, and without the futile-despairing feelings. By now she was fully in touch with her extreme resentments toward her husband and her bitchy mother and wanted help in learning how to push them back and stand up for herself and her individuality. We cut down the sessions to about three the following week and to one or two after that. By the end of the third or fourth week she got a job selling books and was considering taking some classes. She was on the verge of contacting her aggressivity. As she improved and started standing up for her own rights, her husband and mother got more and more belligerent and disturbed and her husband insisted that she stop treatment. Since her depression was gone and she was going in a self-assertive direction and liking herself more, she agreed to stop at that time.

Now—pray tell, how does killing a person's brain cells get them to stand on their own two feet and get them to take care of their needs? How many more patients will be victimized by electric shock treatment before an end is put to this horror, this ludicrous death-dealing horror?

For years I've had the idea that as a last resort in severe suicidal depression, the best bet would be to dangle the person out of the thirteenth-floor window of a building. This life-threatening measure would shock him into an awareness of his life's flow, the adrenal alarm system working to its maximum to keep the person alive, and aware, vital . . . without the loss of a single brain cell.

Hey—are you depressed?—avoid the grand executioner-psychiatrist who will put your brain in his electric chair and at the flick of a button kill a very essential part of you. Yell, scream, beat your couch, punch your husband (or wife) or mother (or in-law)—at least if you're thrown in jail for assault it's *you* doing the assaulting . . . don't let them assault your brain and even pay them for doing it . . . *look to your needs!*

Another depressed and suicidal woman, sixty-five years old, came to see me. She was so agitated and under such great pressure that I found the only way I could get her attention was to yell or at least talk loudly and at the same time tell her not to talk. She had been hospitalized and given shock treatment several times and for the

94

past eight years was given sedatives daily prescribed by her internist.

Soon after the gray-haired woman, Olive, entered my office she began to act crazy, pacing, telling me how sick she felt, that she didn't want to live, that she had had a lot of trouble, that she had been in a state hospital. After a few minutes of hearing her complaints, I told her to shut up, that I didn't want to hear about the past or her troubles, and that if she wanted to live I'd work with her to help her live, and if she wanted to die or wanted drugs or shock treatment, she'd have to leave. She settled down and began to listen to me. Whenever she attempted to interrupt me to tell me about her depression, I told her she was not listening to me and I called her stubborn. She then readily admitted her stubbornness and almost smiled as we talked about this. It seemed that the immediate source of Olive's underlying anger was her forty-year-old daughter who had come to visit her two weeks previously and had dumped her four young kids on Olive while the daughter slept late in the mornings. I immediately sided with Olive, said she had already raised her own kids and done her work and here comes her daughter dumping her kids on her and expecting her to be her housemaid. About ten minutes after the session began I had her beat the couch—she barely patted it, so little force was expressed. I yelled at her in criticism of such poor pounding and yelled my encouragement whenever it seemed her force was increasing somewhat. As she pounded, I yelled at the daughter for taking advantage of Olive and encouraged Olive's expression of her anger toward her daughter. After three or four minutes of pounding, she felt dizzy and exhausted.

Then we sat facing each other and when she attempted again to talk about how depressed she felt, I yelled at her for being stubborn and not listening to me. I repeated again that I didn't want to hear about her sickness, that she'd have to give up her sedative drugs and work my way or I wouldn't work with her. She argued about her need for the sedatives and I compromised, accepting her cutting them in half. I asked her to tune in to her body and give me a measurement of its level of relaxation—she said her whole body was relaxed except for her head which was tight and tense and pressured. I asked her to think of putting her head in my hands (a device I've used for getting the patient to project the disturbing part out and away from the rest of the body . . . which often works miraculously), but she took me literally and leaned her head toward my outstretched palms. So I took her head in my hands, pressed firmly into her scalp and told her to let the tension flow into my hands. After a few minutes, she sat up and again readied herself for a dissertation of her manifold ills. I again yelled at her, pointed out how stubborn she was, and that she wasn't following my recommendation. She seemed to calm down then, becoming less agitated. At one point she asked: "But why don't I want to see people—I used to be so sociable." I answered: "Because you're angry at them . . . you're too angry at them . . . why should you want to see them when you're so angry at them?"

Accepting her stubbornness and encouraging her anger and establishing some physical contact seemed to break through her wall of futility somewhat. My prescription for her was a firm request to stay out of bed during the day, walk outside and keep walking until she was ready to drop, and beat her bed several times a day. Her pacing was not walking, and I told her I didn't want her to do that but to go out of the house and walk. I gave her husband this prescription and he agreed to cooperate. When she left that session she was evidently less agitated, though still depressed. She seemed, too, somewhat more hopeful. I don't know, however, the end of this story for later that evening a doctor in her family insisted she go into a hospital to get shock treatment and I never heard from her again.

And what about lobotomy? We don't hear very much about it these days, and many people-psychotherapists believe it to be passé, a former blot on the escutcheon rubbed out long before the 1970s. Now it is true that lobotomies are not as prevalent anymore . . . but lest anyone have the mistaken idea that the dread lobotomy is dead, I refer them to a presentation by a doctor from New Orleans under the auspices of the Southern Medical Association given in

Miami in November 1971. His talk was entitled: "Stereotaxic Cingulotomy and Prefrontal Lobotomy in Mental Disease." The program notes read as follows: "Prefrontal lobotomy still holds some hope of amelioration of symptoms in mental diseases which have been intractable to all other methods of treatment. A new surgical technique on ten patients yielded excellent results in eight, fair in one and failure in one."

So the symptoms are alleviated, and the patient is at the same time relieved of his essential humanity. Grotesque!—that this dehumanization is considered an "excellent result." And get that audacious and phony "intractable to all other methods of treatment"! What "other methods" were used, I want to know . . . the usual two-second "good morning" therapy routine that the average patient in the chronic psychiatric hospital gets (and rarely any more)? What real therapeutic attempts were made to humanly reach each of these ten vegetables while they were yet troubled human beings?

Do you want to get excellent results for "intractable symptoms"? Then find people like John Rosen, M.D., or Tom Stampfl, Ph.D., who *really* get excellent results . . . mostly from being human with their human patients, getting inside their brains in a reaching, human, encountering way, which has nothing to do with electricity or cutting. If I ever wind up as a patient on the back ward of a psychiatric hospital somewhere, I hope one of these two men or their like will doctor me so I can be brought back to my human functioning again. Keep those cutters, sadists, shockers, ablators away from me and my brain tissue, please, so I can maintain my humanity. And you'd do well to keep them away from yours.

The *New York Post,* on March 10, 1972, reported on "Lobotomies Performed on Five-Year-Olds," and quoted Dr. Peter Breggin, a Washington, D.C., psychiatrist as saying that lobotomies, "brain mutilations," are being performed by American neurosurgeons on four hundred to six hundred people a year to control aggressive behavior, many on hyperactive children, and mostly on women in their forties and fifties. There were fifty thousand victims

97

of lobotomy about twenty to thirty years ago, decreasing in the late fifties, and Dr. Breggin claims we are just at the beginning of a second wave!

Yes, sadism in medicine and neurosurgery and psychiatry is, alas, still rearing its ugly head and destroying human heads in its wake.

My own introduction to modern neurosurgery occurred in my second or third year in medical school—occurred, literally, in one fell swoop, cutting its way into my own brain and leaving the scar even now, some twenty years later.

I refer to the transorbital lobotomy, otherwise known as the ice pick operation. Techniques of this wounding were perfected to such a degree that all that was required was an ice pick-like instrument—no sutures, no bandages—internal bleeding and destruction of nerve pathways and irrevocable death of brain cells with just a thrust of the ice pick . . . and all that's evident on the outside are two black eyes—that clear up in time—and memory loss—that doesn't clear up so well . . . and a state of docile vegetation —that goes on forever. With a flick of the wrist the animal gets changed into a plant—modern alchemy!

My medical school class was invited to see a demonstration of such a transorbital lobotomy, one of several types of lobotomies. The neurosurgeon, on the staff of a university medical school, stood before the class strutting in a sedate, self-important manner. I remember how good looking and smooth he appeared, a typical Hollywood symbol of the handsome doctor whose patients go ga-ga over him . . . and how entirely devoid of character he was. He was meticulously groomed, hair perfectly in place, skin very white and smooth shaven—a perfect, successful representative of White Anglo-Saxon America. He wore a suit and tie and looked as if he were addressing a businessmen's luncheon meeting of the Kiwanis Club. After some introductory remarks he opened the door and the nurse and orderly pushed a stretcher into the room. Walking in with them was an attractive young black man, eighteen years old, looking frightened and bewildered. The neurosurgeon paid no attention to him but continued discussing with us how the operation would be conducted, and he seemed proud of the fact that they didn't even need anesthesia for the operation—that knocking the patient out with "a couple of electric shock treatments would be adequate anesthetization." (I guess when you're contemplating slashing up the brain substance, a little cell damage more or less is not too relevant.)

The young black man in wrinkled hospital garb stood cowering in the corner in sharp contrast with the urbane, smooth, self-possessed, polished physician. Finally the doctor turned to the patient, mentioned briefly his diagnosis . . . Schizophrenic Reaction . . . and that he was a recent hospital admission . . . and told him to get up on the stretcher. The young man backed up, his shoulders hunched like a scared cat being attacked by a growling bulldog, his eyes darting this way and that in a futile attempt to seek some way of escape from the inevitable. The nurse and orderly then held his arms, brought him to the stretcher, and somehow managed to get him to lie down on it, shackling his wrists and ankles. The doctor applied the electrodes to the young man's temples, the current was turned on, and the young man's body jerked convulsively for several seconds. The doctor said smoothly, as though nothing had just happened, that he thought he'd give another dose of electric current to be sure he's knocked out completely. Again the current was turned on, again the captured victim was convulsively responding with his entire body to the electricity searing his brain cells.

(This patient—if he were not poor, not black, not welfare-experimental-animal material—what treatment would then have been meted out to him? . . . need one ask such an obvious question? What treatment for this young black man had he been in the doctor's own family, for instance? *This is the criterion.* If you treat me, no matter who I am, in any way different from the way you would treat your family members and colleagues and peers, then you don't deserve to be in a service profession—get out and get into business! In business you treat everyone with equal contempt, independent of their blood relationship to you—business is business. So get out of the service and helping professions, you doctors, educators, priests, et al. who would dehumanize us—get into the material world—unadulteratedly corrupt—and practice your corruptions on my pocketbook but not on my flesh, my intellect, my spirit!)

I find it very difficult to get back to and face that patient who has just had his second electroconvulsive assault. Since leaving him there I have just now busied myself with phone calls, checking my calendar, eating a homemade milk-and-honey popsicle, and just plain vacating my mind and floating for a while. The subsequent scene is so horrible not only in itself but in all its ramifications that I've been avoiding delving in and confronting it.

Well, back again—the patient was, after the second electric shock, completely limp and "anesthetized." (I have never, neither before nor since that incident, heard of using electricity for anesthesia!) The surgeon then took an instrument *from his pocket* in a pointedly and overly nonchalant manner and showed the ice-pick-like tool to the class. He then lifted one eyelid of the patient's and stuck the pick up—he made a point of showing that he was having some trouble getting the pick through the skull and into the brain at the first try and he grimaced at the class and said something about the "thickness of the boy's skull." A few of the more obvious racists in the class gave him his anticipated reply by snickering—some of the students, already uncomfortable, had their discomfort increased at this remark. After the pick penetrated the skull, he flicked his wrist back and forth with the pick slashing into the brain substance, severing forever, in an instant, those connections that nature had labored to achieve over millions of years. The Brain-Killer, named Neurosurgeon, repeated the ceremony via the patient's other eye socket.

I was not the only one who gasped at the outrage I had just witnessed. One girl, Dottie, her head probably full of all the sterile operative techniques with sterilization of instruments we'd been taught to observe prior to and during any operation, raised her hand and asked about using an unsterilized instrument, to which the surgeon retorted with a pretty-boy smile: "Well, I didn't wipe it on my bootstrap."

Who was there to raise the bigger question—by what right had this surgeon, knowing almost nothing about the patient except that he was black, eighteen, on welfare, and a new hospital admission, butchered this young man's brain for the elucidation of a class of young doctors-to-be? *Who were all those responsible for all the steps required to bring that patient's brain in contact with that butcher's ice pick?*

The show was over—the showman strutted in front of the room, titillated at his own performance—at the suave, nonchalant way he imposed a gruesome spectacle on a class of horrified doctors-to-be.

The young man, never to be whole again, lying stretched out before us, was wheeled out of the room, out of most of our lives. He will always be part of mine—seared forever in my brain, in my guts.

May, as Goethe promised, that pain be halved now that I've shared it with you . . . may the load of it be lighter for me. It will never be lighter for that young man—he is beyond weights and measures—beyond the pain of butcheries—*vegetables don't cry.*

5

ANIMAL
OR VEGETABLE?

The neurosurgeon with his ice pick is an extreme end process; how do people in their day-to-day lives deny their animal vitals and lead themselves to vegetative decay? Yes, even though the neurosurgeons, psychiatrists, medical doctors, and drug companies ply their vegetizing wares, they are not to be wholly blamed for the ravaging of our life flow. Most people in our culture are pill happy, conking out their life experiencing and turning their creative urges into the makings of a human-vegetable garden.

One big difference between animals and vegetables is movement . . . m-o-v-e-m-e-n-t . . . vegetables are mostly rooted, staying in one place . . . no locomotion . . . (remember the psychoanalyst with his ass rooted to his leather chair?) . . . they just absorb anything—any nutrient—that happens to contact their roots . . . they're passive . . . pass-sieve almost . . . accepting anything that comes to them . . . (like your TV dinner on your TV tray brought to you while you're rooted there in front of your TV set). Is there any difference between a vegetable . . . its vege-

103

tativeness . . . and the way millions of Americans spend hours each day in motionless rootedness in front of their TV sets?—nothing going out, except for respiratory and other gases . . . absorbing all that comes to them.

As I write this, I sit at my window desk testing out my own rootedness . . . I look out at the ocean . . . aware of movement . . . my eye hits a bird on the building across the way . . . hits the ocean . . . back to the bird . . . the bird flies away . . . the building without the bird is dull and *I move* my eye back to the ocean . . . I do the moving . . . (I am autonomous) . . . up the beach to the fishing pier . . . to the surfers . . . to the resting folks sunning themselves . . . to the moving sea gulls. I make a decision to move, and I move the scene . . . each movement of mine changes the scene—and I change with it. I'm an animal examing my environment . . . actively . . . though I'm sitting still. I'd be even more participating in my environment if I were out there on the pier . . . or battling the waves . . . or walking the sands. I am in touch with me and my connection with out there. I feel the movement and want *to move*—I now wrestle with my stillness.

When I sit in front of the TV, the vegetable maker, someone else decides my movement for me, where my head should turn, where my eyes should focus. As I remain sitting there, my body and attention rooted, I give up my autonomy. The TV becomes my leader and phototropically I turn to its light, rooted to my appointed spot.

The vegetabilization process begins as early as infancy, and here's the end-product, the vegetable disguised as person who day/night after day/night vibrates to the TV tune in imperceptible mobility . . . in perceptible immobility. Hey!—you want to have an anxiety attack?—just let your picture tube go out of whack . . . wow! —what frenzied calls to the repair man . . . it's almost an emergency . . . it *is* an emergency! And the aimlessness, the restlessness you feel when your Great God TV is not there for your use . . . for your obeisance . . . the fights in families over who's gonna watch what program! The TV has become the New Family Mem-

ber—honored and revered above all others . . . the only one, in
fact, listened to!

Meanwhile . . . back at the ranch . . . the juices of the inner
resources are drying up, the dependency on the outer source becoming greater and greater—

TV, rain on me . . . reign me . . . without you I am arid . . .
I need to suck at your source.

A few years ago I went to a Friday evening discussion party
given by Radio Station KPFK in Los Angeles—the topic was "Uto-
pias." In the crowd there were two smiling "nice" guys—did you
ever see the kind of smiling face whose energy is really drained
out of it, with all the energy remnants going to keeping the smile
pasted on . . . the down mood dimly showing around the edges
of the smile and in the dullness of the eyes? Well, that was these
two guys . . . they didn't look alike in physical dimensions and yet
they were like a pair of Siamese twins . . . and they seemed to
cling to each other for support. They made it known that they were
bachelors and available . . . available for what? . . . posing for
a death mask? They were somewhere in their mid-thirties . . . the
age, at least, was right . . . right for what? One of them in particular was dogging me with questions like: "How come you look
so happy . . . you seem to be enjoying yourself so much?" . . .
anything beyond death row would have looked happy compared to
that guy's real mirror image . . . and we got into a discussion of
"life." I had more patience for bullshitty philosophizing in those
days . . . it was before the great here and now of Gestalt and
Existentialism discovered me. He was asking me for a formula—a
how-to-do-it in 1-2-3 easy lessons. He didn't know that I was a
psychiatrist or he would really have stuck on then. (At parties I
refuse to introduce my title. I go as a person to meet with other
persons hopefully—not statuses or titles. To defend myself against
the status mongers and their sudden phony adulating smile when
they find out you're a doctor-lawyer-Indian chief instead of Joe
Blow, laborer . . . I've hit on an answer to their usual cocktail
party question: What do you do? I look them in the eye, smiling

to take off the sting, and say: "I breathe," which offends some status mongers and amuses those souls who, like me, are bored with stereotyping by status, categorizing by work level.) Sometimes, I'm less devious and therefore more devious and I simply anwer: "I work in an office"—they don't get so antagonistic with this . . . in America, if you're female, you're supposed to be an office worker, a waitress, a housekeeper. (Do men doing office work also accept this stereotype and feel apologetic about working in a "female" role?)

Back to Lack-Luster at the party asking me to give him a simple equation for living. I looked him straight in the eye and said: "Well, the first thing you could do is turn off your television set." He got a sudden look of amazement and almost gasped: "How did you know?"

(Dammit, man, you live in America, don't you? What else do you do in this culture night after night? I'm not clairvoyant . . . I just have to walk through any neighborhood anywhere in America . . . from the slums to the penthouses to the farmlands and see that supra city of metal arms rising up into the sky—metal robots bringing in the robotizing material that glues you to your living room seat . . . or sofa . . . or bed. How many of you repeat the pattern of a former patient I had who, after a hard day's work in construction, would come home to flop before the TV set and, in order that his wife not miss what was happening on television he would haphazardly make sexual advances to her and ultimately, when she permitted, have haphazard intercourse with her, lying on the couch, with the TV within visual and auditory range, flowing over them with greater intensity than any energy, sexual or otherwise, flowing out of those two flaccid bodies. At the onset of treatment, needless to say, his wife was frigid and he had erectile difficulties. But those steel arms, rigid and erect, rose above their home conducting in straight lines their relentless symphony. Listen, man, tear the damn antennas down, and look to your own antenna hanging over, limp, and get anxious, get bored and restless . . . and overcome . . . and live!)

106

OK . . . back to Milky-Toast and the party . . . he told me that as soon as he came home from work as an accountant (office work!) he would turn the TV on . . . he had almost no male friends, no female friends at all, and spent almost every evening before the TV set. When he went out during the week he'd go to visit his "twin" and they'd watch TV together.

I shrugged, ready to give up in despair of ever communicating my reaction to such waste, but he persisted in attempting to follow me: "You mean I should just turn it off?" He looked incredulous . . . such a daring thought had never occurred to him . . . and his hand shot out in an involuntary gesture simulating turning the TV knob. Then suddenly the awareness of what I was suggesting seemed to hit him all at once . . . it was as if he had at that moment been in face to face confrontation with the ghost of himself . . . its pale lifeless shadow . . . and his face dropped its party facade and for the first time looked real . . . and in trouble. Slowly . . . falteringly . . . the words emerged: "But what do I do then?" And there was his hopelessness, his futility, allowed a moment's emergence on his face . . . and by the time I said: "You'd find out then what to do," he was already submerged, defended, smoothly smiling, buried, and dead.

I was so struck by this caricaturelike incident . . . so tormented by all the things growing and ceasing to grow beneath the scene I had just witnessed and been part of . . . that shortly thereafter I began writing my play, *The Drugstore,* in which I placed these two hollow men. They helped me deal with the theme of America as a vast drugstore. And I suppose it's a heavy theme to me, for here I am still carrying it around, trying to deal it out to you and so share it.

Well, before I leave the Lord TV and those idolatrous hollow men "leaning together, headpieces filled with straw" . . . before I leave the all-American family sitting before their God, the whole family down to the three-year-olds sitting in rapt attention while someone's telling them what deodorant to use in order to get people to like them . . . with Julia in my play I cry out to those family members:

"Oh, look around your room, you foolish people! Who's liking you *now?* Which of those glued eyes and brains surrounding you has anything left over to like you with—no matter how much deodorant you pour on?"

Look, I'm not saying we should get rid of TV altogether. I think it does have potential for enriching our lives culturally and educationally and aesthetically, I think it can move us to exciting, constructive action. It's when we and the TV producers (with their ugly profit motive) use it to pacify our boredom and loneliness that it becomes such a damaging, vegetabilizing device.

All right—good-bye to TV darkness, which robs me of my animal sightedness, and hello to the light of infancy. A quick hello before it, too, yields to darkness and vegetabilization. The newborn infant— the whole world and he are one . . . the world is his extension. A hunger cry brings (should bring, I mean) the mother's breast, which he perceives as an extension of himself. This, our earliest magic: I cry—a bulging breast appears, its oozing nipple enters my mouth, and my cry is appeased. As every woman knows who has nursed her baby and not outraged her and her baby's nature with the damming back properties of stilbestrol (another hormonal stifler—stifling the breasts and the mother's natural surges . . . stifling the baby's natural urges . . . the only urging evidenced in the stilbestrol scene is that of the doctor "encouraging" the mother to use an "easy substitute"), as every nursing mother knows, at the sound of the infant's hunger cry the breast has a feeling of a sudden rush, the "letting down" of the milk, it fills up, ballooning out, the nipple gets erected, and milk starts oozing or even gushing out . . . all this occurring at the dimmest hunger cry even though the infant may be two or three rooms away. And wow!—what a tremendous feeling this is . . . indescribable!—a mother in touch with her own natural flow and her infant's! A mother in touch with herself can distinguish between a hunger cry and a cry for attention, fretfulness, discomfort, playfulness, or just plain orneriness. And if she's not sure about the hunger cry, all she has to do is to tune in to what her breasts are telling her. What a fabulous superradar system: infant's stomach (hunger pain) → infant's cry → mother's breast → mother's milk → and everybody's happy. No vegetables here in this kingdom of the animal!

Do you know the fantastic joy of holding your newborn snuggled against your breast, of feeling your milk gurgling into its wrinkled chicken skin body—filling out and smoothing out the wrinkles, padding the fat pads of your baby's cheeks, feeling the tensions relax as the baby's gut gets filled with warm body-temperature milk from your body: *Nature's natural transfusion.* God! When I think of the ridiculous experiments created and performed by American (not Nazi) doctors giving refrigerator-temperature milk to babies with the doctors' scientific conclusions assuring us that the babies thrive just as well with the frigid milk! *Thrive?* What measures this "thrive"—height and weight? Where's the "thrive" measurement in the baby's . . . what's the word for it? . . . psyche, gut, marrow, id, core—I don't know . . . spirit maybe . . . in the baby's person—the animal person, the beautiful natural animal longing for its mother's milk from its mother's body, from its mother's tit, *direct,* with no middlemen. Who measures what happens when this is denied? . . . what measure for *this* kind of deprivation! The gauleiter men or women— the "doctors" who devised this special form of deprivation of newborns are like the doctors who deprive uncertain new mothers of the encouragement to nurse their babies by the propaganda that it's easier, more efficient, to bottle feed, and anyone can be substituted for the mother: a nurse, a neighbor, a paid employee, even a pillow prop. What a substitute culture we're living in! Hey, you wanna get really *daring?* Why not try the *real thing?*

Listen—the best fulfiller in the whole world when you're two days old is your mama's warm tit and when you're twenty-two it's your peer-mama's hot twat (that is, if you've graduated from the oral zone to other more functional and fitting places and parts). Why is this obvious truth decked out in masks and subterfuge? What's

109

the whole world about anyway, if not for life and death. That *is* the world: Life and Death. Life's continuity depends on procreation. Ergo, it follows as the night the day, life and sex are intimately united—are one. So's death.

About death—there's a beautiful little play by Brian Friel called *Lovers,* which shows two young students in love, and the commentary interspersed in the play tells of their death while the audience is still seeing them argue about whose family will do what after they are married, reaching an intensity of ferocity when they talk about in-law troubles, and here they are but teen-agers. The audience knows that on their way back to town from their mountain rendezvous they will die by drowning. The juxtaposition of the petty, picayune quarreling with the knowledge of their imminent death had a powerful impact on me. Similarly I remember a couple in my office, the woman slowly dying of cancer, and the petty, trifling fights she and her husband were having, while the underlying poignant theme of her death and its leaving young children without a mother was never once touched by them. Hey! Wake up! Make it as a person first before you make it as a corpse.

> Oh, Here and Now:
> To you I bow . . .
> I take this vow:
> To plow . . . to plow.

Here in my guts is my life. These external accouterments, my possessions, my dwelling, are burdens on my back . . . the less of them I have, the less I have to bowl me over with and conceal my gut, the lighter I am, my shoulders back, my gut to the fore, and forward march!

Hey—we're all gonna die: atheists and religionists, communists and capitalists and anarchists, scientists and mystics, status holders and have-nots, smarts and stupids—this is clear. *But not all of us are gonna live!* And if we look for life in our externals (business success, possessions, marital partner, children even) and not in our internals, we stay dead till our heart stops. What a horrendous waste! And you don't have to live on a commune to get in touch with your guts. In fact, if communal living means getting out of yourself with pot, you're already dead. About gut—

Dear Gut: hello—I'm thrilled to meet you . . . you make me feel so alive, so quivery . . . I want to stay close to you always till death do us part. When I'm in touch with you I feel electric—I don't have to stuff my mouth and fill you up, don't have to smoke or chew, don't have to be wordy and smart, don't have to drug myself into other experiencing . . . I am jealous of anything that keeps me from you . . . and why don't these poor doped-up bastards putting themselves to sleep see how great is the power in their guts? Wow, I can explode the world (that is, its mythology within myself) when I'm in touch with you. It's when I lose you that the myths conk me out and I'm a wiped-out zombie. Hey, Gut—I'm thrilled with you and I'm staying close. I can plow and be plowed if I stay with you here and now. How my field grows!

. . . Now that I've gotten into my gut I feel very loving to all of you—even to the red-necked older guy in Flamingo Park last week who almost had apoplexy when I said we were perpetrating genocide in Vietnam. "Where'd you get that idea!" he shouted, getting very red . . . "I never heard of that!" . . . I asked him if he had ever heard about racism in America where we have racism and all that. He yelled as he quickly walked away from me (my hostile vibrations were more than he could stand, to say nothing of his own): "You probably even like Malcolm X!" "Yes," I said excitedly, "you're right—I love that guy—he's great!"

Yes, right now I can smile, love myself, and even love that gentleman in the park who talked of carrying a gun with him to protect himself—I'd be his first victim before he'd turn on my black brothers—right now, in touch with my own humanity, I can feel and appreciate his, warped though its expressions were. (Don't expect this mood to last . . . I'm not a Christ figure, far from it

. . . but I have my moments of enlightenment. Though I may never, after this moment, feel so kindly toward that gentleman again.)

Yes, it's when I stay in touch with my gut reactions and avoid substitutes for living and feeling that I can ward off the decaying process. It's hard to live a real life in a profit-pushing ersatz culture, but the struggle keeps me alive. My struggle to stay with the real sometimes takes me to extremes in warding off the ersatz. Like, I'm a sucker for the word "natural"—there's something in this symbol that makes me recklessly buy anything that has this label—I don't know how "natural Cheddar cheese" differs from just plain Cheddar cheese, but I'll spend an extra half buck on the natural one because of my enamored state. Will someone please explain the difference? And I don't know why prunes in a health food store without preservatives are twice as expensive as prunes in a supermarket *with* preservatives . . . besides, who needs prunes anyway? If I take care of my gut by staying in touch with its aliveness and electricity it won't hold back on me—it will daily give up its yield voluntarily and spontaneously, without any extraneous pushing.

Natural—while we're on this subject, I had a patient, a forty-year-old commercial artist with a rigid, Southern Baptist background who was suffering from impotence. (Can we say that the more rigid your background, the less rigid your foreground?)

In one of our sessions early in treatment, I became impressed suddenly with the rigid, immobile mask he was wearing. As I focused on his stony facial musculature, I began to feel my own face muscles tighten up. They became so uncomfortable, I began to move my face around vigorously, squinting, grimacing, opening my mouth very wide, opening my eyes like moons . . . moving my facial muscles in every which way possible; and I invited him to join me. He began very hesitantly to move his facial muscles . . . almost imperceptibly . . . whereupon I made some really weird, ugly faces full of grotesque movements and told him to move more. As he continued to move his face more and more, he began to drop the masklike facial expression with the veiled eyes . . . and began to allow himself to just *be*. At one point, when he was looser than I'd ever seen him before, and while he was simply breathing deeply and contacting his feelings (*not* his thoughts or concepts or ideologies or past histories!), this impotent man blurted out: *"It feels so unnatural to be natural!"*

Imagine! And recall the horrified young woman who felt nursing a baby to be such an unnatural act!

Speaking of impotence, a patient who suffered temporary impotence while his wife became more and more withdrawn and cold to his sexual overtures entered treatment at a time when his marriage was at a breaking point. Both husband and wife exhibited similar inability to deal directly with their anger toward each other. The wife, Arline, either literally walked away from confrontation with her husband or became withdrawn to the point where even her voice emerged as a bare whisper. On some level each feared not only the other's anger but also the possible murderous effects of his or her own anger on the other. In working with them individually at one point, I presented them with a fantasy trip incorporating their fears of killing and being killed.

For example, in dealing with Arline's fear of her husband it evolved that she really was afraid he could kill her. She had lived with this dim fear for the eighteen years of their marriage. So in our session I suggested she follow a fantasy trip that I spontaneously devised for her, with her help, blow by blow in which her husband attacked her, brutalized her sexually, battered her with his fists, then cut her up with a knife—blood was spurting out from all over her macerated flesh when finally he plunged the knife into her heart and in a geyser of blood she gave up the ghost and was dead. Throughout this fantasy she was visibly tense, her face contorted in apparent anguish and she seemed to be experiencing the horror of the scene as I described it. At the end, after she was "dead," she visibly relaxed and her face looked peaceful. I asked: "What are you feeling now, Arline?" She smiled faintly, eyes still closed, and said in a soft voice: "Calm . . . relaxed . . . at peace." "Good," I said, "just let yourself enjoy that feeling." She remained that way

113

for several minutes and seemed reluctant to give up the state. The session had a profound effect of reversing her fear of her husband's violence, and for the first time in many months she approached him with relative calm. In the next session I led her on a fantasy trip playing out her murderous feelings toward her husband.

E: Now visualize yourself in a room with your husband, and you're angry. How could you show your anger?

A: I could walk out. (Typical of her past behavior.)

E: How else?

A: I could yell at him.

E: How could you hurt him?

A: I guess I could slap him.

E: Yes! . . . do that. See yourself doing that. He is so stunned he just stands there while you slap him. What do you feel now?

A: I feel wonderful . . . I feel ten feet tall.

E: Feel ten feet tall. Feel how good it is to be ten feet tall. He's just a pygmy now and you can do whatever you want with him. How else can you hurt him?

A: I could scratch him.

E: Yes—scratch him. See that. See yourself scratching his face . . . see the blood coming out . . . scratch at his eyes . . . feel your nails digging into his flesh, his eyeballs—you're scratching his eyes out. Now what else could you use besides your nails and your hands to hurt him with?

A: I could use my feet and kick him.

E: Yes—where could you kick him to hurt him the most?

A: (Smiles somewhat shamefacedly) In the groin.

E: Yes—do that. Kick him in the balls—you really got him that time—you knocked the breath out of him. He's doubled over in pain—you kick him in the stomach and knock him down. See that. (Pause) Now what else can you use to hurt him with?

A: My teeth—I could bite him.

E: Yes, do that. See yourself biting him—bite his ears, feel that flesh and cartilage between your teeth, clenching your jaws and wrenching the ears from his head . . . bite his nose until it be-

114

comes a pulpy mass. Now start on his penis—he'll be sorry he ever started with you—just get that penis in your mouth and bite it, wrench it off. And now do the same with his balls—feel that. You're really going to give it to him this time. Feel that. And now you dig those nails into his chest, rip his flesh off, feel those ribs cracking. You tear open his chest cavity and grab his heart in your hands and you bite into it and suck the blood out of it. Feel that. And now he's finished—he's not going to hurt you any more. Feel that. (Pause) And now what are you feeling?

A: (Smiles, relaxed, stretches arms up in the air) I feel great— I feel ten feet tall.

E: Feel that—feel how it feels to be ten feet tall. Enjoy that feeling.

Arline's husband had similar sessions confronting his anger toward his wife and also his fear of her anger. Following these sessions, and for the first time in their relationship, they were able to discuss some extremely difficult problems without panic or rage reactions, and their sexual experience with each other began to improve to the point of his having increased staying powers and his wife's having orgasm during intercourse, whereas she previously had experienced orgasm only by manual manipulation.

Well—back to my consideration of natural things.

Hello—I'm back damning the substitutes in ersatz America—I can't seem to escape them anywhere. In June 1970 I was in Los Angeles having gone to California to attend a professional workshop, and look—I go to my friend's house there and see this bottle of orange juice, I think, sitting in her refrigerator and I thirstily reach in and pour myself out a luscious-looking glassful. Then I look at the label . . . *disgusting!* The inviting orange liquid has a life-repellant label that reads: *Orange juice blend* . . . contains at least 70% orange juice from frozen concentrated orange and orange juice, water, sweeteners (the kind that ruin your and my kidneys?), citric acid (another preservative to pollute the rivers and streams of my blood-circulating system), orange emulsion (whatever the hell that means), and ascorbic acid (from an ersatz source?) . . .

115

Wow!—all I want is simple orange juice, just the way it comes from the orange . . . the real thing. Christ!—can't I get the *real thing* anywhere in America?

I was just thinking about water—a great discovery as a drink. Fantastic. Who ever stops to get the real thing for thirst—when there's the poisoned variety leering down at us from billboards, bombarding us from our television sets and radios . . . the Coca-Colas, Pepsi-Colas, diet drinks, coffee, tea, cocoa, and all other such junky poisonous substitutes. Damnit—rediscover the real thing —face the damn withdrawal symptoms for a few days and get back to reality. Big discovery—Water Quenches Thirst—a great drink— for real! And hurry, before the pollutants catch up and ruin the last great drink there is.

Where are our country's real schools and real teachers? One aspect of the revolution taking place in America is what's happening in the fertile oases scattered here and there amidst the desert schools, oases where students help make up the school curriculum, give their teachers ratings and suggestions for classroom work, and have some voice in administrative matters.

But our average schools and teachers—oh, how arid! While schools of fish go slipping through the deep, following their instincts and their destiny . . . schools of students go plodding through their classes, closing off their instincts, denying their destiny and hampering it from ever taking place. Our students in our death-giving schools—not so fortunate as fish . . . not so vital even as a *vegetable!* A plant takes in sunlight and water and minerals and creates organic compounds—vegetables alter in their substance what comes into them. Yes—even the vegetable alters what comes into it! Not so the students of our mass-produced, factory-modeled schools and universities operating on the funnel system. The teachers or professors pour the predigested, ready-made, processed stuff into a funnel that empties into the mass of students before them . . . the students in turn are expected to deliver up the stuff, *unchanged,* back to the teachers . . . utterly unchanged in any individualizing process . . . the teachers, likewise, remaining un-

116

changed. *Students aren't even supposed to be vegetables!* Any originality, individuality, creativity, or deviation from the processed, funneled-in material that gets funneled directly back to the professors is not only discouraged but penalized. If the answers are not exact replicas, then the poor professors have to use some brain processes on the material and this will never do in a computerized, mechanized, robotized system—it would really jam up the works. Why, if some student emerged, not too far, just, let us say, to a vegetable level—and let us not forget, vegetables don't even cry— then the process of altering what comes in from the professor's outpouring might produce such a dangerous product as to explode the whole IBM system altogether! If you have any doubts about the clear-cut materialistic decay of our educational system, I remind you of the national sales of term papers and Ph.D. theses sweeping our country . . . it's become big business, a supermarket of term papers.

So, let us not disdain the lowly vegetable—it has more power for changing than these, the highest of our nation's students, are allowed to have, safely ensconced at the other side of our massive funnel.

Funnel it in, funnel it out—hurray for such scholarship—it keeps the wheels rolling, the bombs dropping, the kids from crying.

Wait a minute, though . . . all teachers are not funnelizers. Some are crazy enough to be human. There are oases in the desert after all—where green things grow.

A fifteen-year-old high school student, Lenny, who recently started treatment, told me that he was getting an A in his math course and that for the past several years he had been getting F's. Last year he had had a math tutor, and he still got an F. Immediately restraining myself from putting a feather in my hat by attributing his sudden improvement to my work with him, I asked him what he thought caused his improvement. He said it was the teacher: "I've never had a teacher like that—he jumps up and down and will do anything just to get our attention and keep it. The other day he cracked us up by walking around the room wearing a monocle and talking with a German accent for half an hour. He's a gas."

That creative, human teacher was able to mobilize in this boy interest and achievement in a subject . . . an interest that intensive efforts of a math tutor over an entire year and many other teachers had not ever been able to arouse—simply by *risking being silly and thus human* and allowing his creativity to flow!

One morning I called a friend, a literate English teacher, to get the exact wording of a quote from Rilke's "The Blind Man." (I used to own a marvelous collection of his poems with a beautiful translation, but it's gone like most of my past possessions.) I complained to her that in the main library of Miami Beach there are many books *about* Rilke and *about* his poetry, but not one single poem of his in the entire library! She said: "Yes, well that's all most teachers are interested in, you know—not that you read the poems but that you say the 'right things' about them and read what the authorities say." I mused on this . . . it's like eating predigested food . . . the product of someone else's digestion . . . someone else's vomitus or shit.

Say, English teachers, stop wallowing in by-and-buy-products . . . get to the real thing . . . the essence . . . if your students can get one thrill from one word or one turn of a phrase or flight of poetry, they will enliven you . . . provoke you . . . give you life. Don't require them to deal with someone else's digestive processes. What students need is a shot in the guts from a true artist, not from those tired, pedantic souls who pore over words with their hypertrophied cerebrums and atrophied innards. (Of course, I'm not talking here of critics who are themselves artists, like Cleanth Brooks or Robert Penn Warren or Edmund Wilson, or Lionel Trilling, who can open doors to a creative world and enlighten and enliven the reader.) Don't expect or accept vomitus from your students . . . demand your students' contact with the artist's creation itself . . . the reverberation will resound back through to you . . . your and their spirits will resonate together . . . don't deny yourselves this power. Don't demand ersatz aridities . . . get to the creative spirit. Swing! Sing!

One morning I put in a call to the principal of a high school—

118

a fourteen-year-old patient had cut a couple of classes and was up for suspension from school, and I wanted to talk to this principal before he saw her. (I was used to such cooperative discussions with teachers and principals in the years I worked as school psychiatrist for the New York City Board of Education, Bureau of Child Guidance. Even those principals who were tight and rigid—emperors of their domain—interested in their domination and not in those dominated—at least gave lip service to some interest in the students.) I anticipated talking to him about my patient and expected he'd be glad to share the decision making with another professional . . . I naïvely assumed that his goal would be identical with mine, namely doing what would be in the student's best interests.

Actually, I had a lot of questions about the efficacy of suspending her . . . for one thing she had truanted several times previously without being caught and suspension might act as a deterrent from future goofing off. On the other hand, I had seen her about four times and about one week previously she had begun to show increased interest in her school subjects . . . a suspension might increase her resentment and throw her back into poor school functioning, in addition to her having a permanent mark on her record that might have some negative effect on her later getting into a college of her choice.

This was the seesaw I was on that morning while waiting for the school administrator to get to the phone, hoping that together we could arrive at some decision that would benefit my patient. Did I say his interests were in the direction of what was best for the student? Nothing could have been farther from the truth! I was greeted (put off, rather) by a cold, supercilious, properly dictioned man's voice, the mere tone of which quite clearly indicated that he didn't know why the hell I was calling. "I'll make my decision after I see her and hear the facts. She is probably from a middle-class home and wants her own way and has not had enough restraints put on her . . . I know the type . . . I have an office full of them right now." He was obviously blowing to show me how smart he was . . . one-upmanship . . . how much insight he had,

119

and how busy he was! So where the hell do you come off bothering *me* with this kind of thing?

Instinctively I knew that I had to be polite to the shit or his fragile ego would revenge itself on my patient. And, believe it or not, I was polite . . . and kept my patient unhurt by him, for he did not suspend her. What I did: I asked him if he'd like to call me later after speaking to her and let me know what decision he came to. Now get this for dishonest and galling communication: "I think it would be best if she told you about it herself . . . it would be better for her relationship with you . . . (now here comes the truth) and I have an office full of students, I'm so very busy." Goddamn it . . . no wonder there's so much truanting if vomity guys like this set school policy.

Hey, you punks, you contemptuous school administrators, I sentence you to one day of sitting, gagged, in an arena surrounded by your students and having to listen to everything they have to tell you about yourselves. You'll find your mirror there—the truth you conceal from yourselves. And it will hurt. And it might save you. In facing the pain of ourselves we find salvation.

And while I'm talking about arid schools, teachers, and administrators, I'd like to talk about so-called sex education as it is usually taught in American schools. In the name of progress they're showing films on masturbation . . . sterile, dead films showing, for example, a boy (never a girl, mind you . . . girls in the 1970s still aren't supposed to do or talk about such things) . . . they're showing a boy visiting a clinical team of rigid men, usually old— psychologists and medical doctors. The clinicians, frequently wearing white (sterile, "professional") coats, talk to the boy, their faces barely moving, about the "release of tension" and "nocturnal emissions" . . . talk as though they were giving mathematical formulas that the boy should memorize. Any resemblance between their description of masturbation and the real thing is totally non-existent. What's a boy or girl going to do about pleasurable feelings, guilt feelings, feelings of excitement . . . and no word is ever mentioned in these films about—God forbid!—passion. You edu-

120

cators, sitting in your professorial robes and not in your bodies, where's the guts in all this sex "education"?

Is this the great advance we're fighting for—to get this kind of sex education in the schools? Hey, traditional churchmen, Birchites, members of the Women's Christian Temperance Union, and all you others of the silent majority wielding your weight against progress: you'd do best to support this type of sex education—after all, it's as sterilized as celibacy and abstinence—as infertile as ignorance. Never fear—not one word of passion or pleasure will sully the dutiful, honorable, pedantic purity of this type of presentation—and the grand hypocrisy will persist, namely that parents don't screw, nor do all those parent-substitutes in schools, churches, and governments . . . all those running us (not themselves, though!) in celibate circles. And this hypocritically based mythology helps make the young child, and later the child within the man, feel guilty about his own animal urges while he looks upon all authority figures with awe as being superior to himself in their lack of human frailties.

As a matter of fact, I basically don't think sex can be "taught" in schools or any other place for that matter. The very fact that we feel a natural function has to be "taught" shows already the breakdown of natural functioning in the home. If authority figures, starting with parents, stopped the big deceit and showed themselves as sexual beings . . . and I don't mean they have to screw in front of their kids to do this—in fact, if they do screw in front of their kids in our culture it would probably screw up their kids even more . . . if parents, teachers, preachers were to act as if they too have genitals that function and stop hiding them under symbolic fig leaves, the problem of sexual instruction would be well on its way to solution.

Let's take menstruation for instance. The best thing a mother can do to open her daughter to this natural functioning of the uterus is to start early by letting the little child walk in on her when she's changing her bloody napkin or bloody Tampax . . . and when the child is ready to ask questions, the mother can give

121

her the simple facts of the monthly event, which the child will then accept as naturally as urination, as just another body function . . . and not something to fear and clamp (cramp) up about.

I was once on a university panel discussing sex education. Also on the panel were a minister and a dean, each of whom gave a somewhat pedantic discussion of the subject to a small group composed largely of teachers and teacher supervisors. When it was my turn to speak, I told the group I would not "talk about" anything but rather would attempt to present them with an experience from which they might learn how better to teach the subject to others. I asked them to sit around in a circle, preferably alternating male and female, and suggested that the minister sit between two women. He had been sitting in the one regal chair in the room, the chair being pushed away from contact with the others. He reacted with some resentment at being asked to leave his chair and enter the circle like the others, but followed my suggestion nonetheless. I then asked the group to follow my next suggestion: "Turn to the persons sitting next to you and say, as the case may be, 'I have a penis' or 'I have a vagina.' " Many of these educators became flustered, a few tried to say the words and failed, and the minister said the words but then became very hostile to me and verbally attacked me: "First you made me change my chair, and then you put words in my mouth and made me say them!" I told him that I had suggested some things and that it was *his choice* whether to follow my suggestions or reject them. He sat on the edge of his chair, snapped his fingers in the air, and said: "I always forget that! I'm such a sheep!" and with that his hostility diminished and the group went on to discuss the experiences they had just undergone minus the usual bullshitting pedantry.

I shudder to think of the horrible waste, the human pathos and tragedy in the whole abortion scene that is a logical outcome of the "dutiful" attitude toward sex. I guess if I were a master logician called upon to rationalize the denunciation of abortion, it would go something like this: Sex should be only for procreation, never for recreation . . . if a woman gets pregnant, she validates the procreative nature of the sex act. Ergo, it follows that she must, at all cost, have the baby.

There is something deeply sinister in the oppressive hanging on to inhumane laws and dictates at such great cost to human suffering. Those people—the leaders and administrators of the symphony of human suffering—are the same people who would deny us heartiness in language and who would deny us our individuality in appearance and ideology while they remain tied to a sinister death-bent, dehumanized score.

Words, words—originally developed to facilitate and intensify human interaction or communication; now too often used to confound and stifle it, especially stifling being the words of officialdom. One morning as I was walking my daughter to her kindergarten class, I glanced at the stamped envelope in my hand with the scrawled address of: Dean, Graduate School, H University. This addressed envelope had been enclosed in a letter sent to me by one of my students who had been in my Humanistic Psychology class at the University of Miami. In his letter the student had requested that I write a reference for him to the graduate school. His letter of request:

J. F. S.

Monday

Dear Eileen,

Thanks very much for the change of grade and consenting to be one of my references for graduate school.

H University wanted a reference for application for graduate assistantship and left it all up in the air as to the structuring of the content. I imagine that a usual straightforward type will suffice. Thanks an awful lot again and if you have some free time to get together sometime, I'd like that very much.

Peace—Power to No One

(signed) John

123

And now, enclosed in the scrawled, unprofessional-looking envelope I was holding was the following letter, typed on my professional stationery:

Eileen Walkenstein, M.D.

February 13, 1970

Dean, Graduate School
H University

Dear Sir:

I am pleased to recommend John S. to your graduate school. I know him fairly well through my class at the University of Miami that I taught last term in Humanistic Psychology; I find him to be a most intelligent and sincere person with much integrity. I have had numerous private conversations with John, all of which have fostered my deep respect for him.

Should there be any additional information you may require, please do not hesitate to contact me.

Sincerely yours,
(signed) Eileen Walkenstein, M.D.

As I approached the mailbox, it suddenly occurred to me that the envelope may have been inaccurately addressed and, without a return address, there would be no way of knowing whether the Dean received it. At that moment a man in shirt-sleeves was passing and I quickly noted a pen protruding from his shirt pocket. I borrowed it from him, put my own return address in a scrawling hand with my name and title attached to it and promptly mailed it. Perhaps it was the odd juxtaposition of the scrawled, sort of sloppy-looking envelope with the formal, proper, stiff contents that led me to think over how the letter would have been written had I expressed myself without the formal bullshit of the implacable machine letters on the official stationery ensconced inside but rather with the tenor of the loose, free-swinging handwritten envelope. So . . . it would—or should—or could go like this:

Hi Dean!

I want you to know that I had this groovy cat in my Humanistic Psychology class last term at the University of Miami . . . his name is John S. He's a beautiful guy, blond hair hanging down in corn silk rows below his ears . . . moustache to match . . . looks like a soulful version of one of the three musketeers. And his eyes—man! What eyes—sensitive blue with deep undercurrents like a calm ocean on a sunlit day . . . with eyes like that he doesn't have to fall back on the verbal stuff in order to communicate. His voice . . . masculine, deep, gentle, calm . . . a fitting accompaniment to the eyes' calm. He moves through space with an enviable containment, speaks when necessary with intelligently great economy and softness . . . the strength beneath surfacing continually as if to remind one not to be misled by the gentle film.

(I'm slipping off now into some ethereal language, but come to think of it, John *is* an ethereal kind of guy . . . into Yoga and Zen Buddhism and all that, and moving, nonetheless, with his feet on the ground. He accompanied me on a candlelight peace march at the University of Miami on October 15, 1969, when my entire class decided to join the march instead of staying in the classroom. That particular march, walking quietly with John by my side, holding hands occasionally, was striking to me for its solemnity especially considering the myths about the "wild-eyed youths" on peace marches.)

John's a guy I can trust. We've had some groovy rap sessions and I came out really digging him. If you want to talk with me any more about him, great!

So long for now,
Eileen W.

125

Now, put the two letters to the Dean side by side—the one saying what was "supposed" to be said, the other what I really felt; the one in dead verbiage, the other alive with my feelings and experiences.

Official language is gutless and heartless with its unimpassioned proprieties, its safeness, its goddamned traditional safeness. We accept anything as long as it has its safe stamp of traditionalism. And the thing about it is that we don't even have to think—just get the right mold to fit the right occasion—official language is like buying a birthday card or a condolence card. Nothing offensive . . . nothing touching . . . nothing real. Ersatz sentiments and no one gets touched . . . and we can all remain unmoved and unmoving in our zombie or vegetable state.

As for heartiness and passion in language—let's take "fuck" for instance. It's such a descriptive word when used at certain times in certain places. As with some Yiddishisms, there are no appropriate substitutes or adequate translations. "But it's just used for shock value—it's disgusting!" What's wrong with shock value? If it shocks you into awareness—great! If it shocks you into dying, like the brain cells in electric-shock treatment, yes, *this* is truly disgusting!

Speaking about the word fuck—a while back I was invited to give a poetry reading at a humanist society meeting in a Unitarian church and, among others, I invited a gay divorcée I knew, a woman who had no hesitation swinging gaily in and out of any man's bed as long as he wined and dined her properly and treated her with proper decorum and respect. To my reading she brought her teen-age daughter, aged sixteen I think. Of the thousands of words I spoke through my poems that evening, the one rare word, fuck, stuck in her throat and her brain (like Macbeth's word "Amen" stuck in his throat when he was going to murder the king). She came up to me after the program, visibly disturbed, and vehemently said: "I brought my daughter to hear Culture, to be elevated . . . if I had known it would be pornographic, I would never have brought her. Why the hell didn't you warn me?" See

126

what a hearty word this "fuck" is—not only capable of arousing this woman's anger but of subduing, for her, thousands of other words, of other feelings. For, except for this word, she had missed the whole evening.

And now, let's look at a companion word to "fuck"—a word just about as strong as fuck, as alive in its reverberations, as compelling in its power: the word "schmuck." Is there any word that comes up to it in force, in contempt, in sheer power to flay, to flatten out? "Prick" just doesn't measure up no how. You call a guy a prick and somehow he can still talk to you—you can still be friends. You call him a schmuck—and it's the end of everything—finito—basta—the point of no return.

"You schmuck!" is the dagger thrust to the balls, the penile decapitation, the final blow beyond which there is no more—and you can't ever replace the decapitated head—forever it dangles there in dripping blood and nothing can ever put the pieces together again.

What an epithet! What a word! In the beginning was the word and this is one of those words—the beginning and the end—the be-all and the end-all.

Alas—as "fuck" and "schmuck" become integrated into our common everyday usage they will lose their magnitude, their power, and never again will they ascend to their former supremacy.

Look, you Birchers, Billy Grahams et al.—if you want to rob these words of their power you would do well to foster their usage. Your attack only strengthens their use. Just imagine if a sermon of Billy Graham's were preceded by one dozen fucks and interspersed with three dozen more fucks and if the entire congregation were to join him in a fuck-fuck-fuck-fuck grand unison finale—why, it wouldn't be long before he would have won the battle of the word—hasn't he learned the primitive lesson that if you can't beat them, join them? Does he not see that his battle gives force, power, pungency to the word he attacks—his force creates an equal counterforce? Yes, he must see this—and he must, therefore, love the fuck word he attacks so vehemently—his power is in keeping the power of this adored word alive in all of its ramifications. What a clever mother!

I'm just thinking how I've come to hate some of the popular expressions and two of the worst phrases, which offend me, come immediately to mind—"do your own thing" and "tell it like it is." When I hear these phrases as part of a natural flow of street language with the appropriate dialect connected with them, they flow okay . . . and I feel accepting. On the other hand, when I hear them come from a stiff-collared, properly dictioned Madison Avenue type, I feel like vomiting, that is, when my boredom allows me sufficient feeling to react at all.

And Jesus!—that's what's so great about the word fuck—it's entirely unsullied by contamination with the establishment—you never hear the President of the United States in a press interview talking about the "fucking protestors" or blasting a "fuck you!" to the Russians. As long as it stays outside the establishment, it keeps its vibrancy alive, its power for human impact vital.

So please, Mr. Nixon and Mr. Graham, keep your language *clean* so that I can keep my language alive. Thank you, sirs.

> How comfortable to be a vegetable . . .
> > but how dull . . .
> > yet how safe and predictable.

> How anxietied to be a human animal . . .
> > but how exciting . . .
> > yet how risky and unpredictable.

Revelations

> People who worry about words like fuck
> seem to take nicely to war and the muck
> connected thereto and ask for more:
> More, More . . . Bigger, Better, Muckier War!

People who worry out of proportion
whenever we loosen the laws of abortion
delight in tightening the hub
of Law and Order with Mace and Club.

And those who throw such coarse invectives
at popularizing contraceptives
will readily condone and be most receptive
to cigarette advertising's directives.

And those who 'gainst long hair, pot, and acid rail
and want to throw all hips in jail
are the same who trip right out of life
with booze, barbs, tranquilizers, and marital strife.

We are so simply predictable, despite our sham—
Tell me your views of Vietnam,
             I'll reveal to you what you feel
                 for man.

6

CRIPPLING THE KID
OR THE EARLY MAKINGS
OF A VEGETABLE

In the beginning was—the newborn infant who is the true Buddhist:

> I am in everything . . .
> Everything is in me.

At his birth, the infant takes the whole world as his worth. And now, hello again to the light of infancy—and to that infant while he is yet in his pristine human animal state.

As I've said, the most perfect fulfiller for the infant is the breast with its built-in mechanism for control of the milk supply, with its connections with mama's warm body and embracing arms and feeling flow. It's not just the milk flowing into the baby's body, it's the feeling too that's nourishing him. And besides the stomach hunger, what he screams for, what he wants, what he needs is to be held, body to body . . . he absolutely needs this for both emotional and also physical growth. How clever we are that we can fool the infant with a substitute, that when he wants warm soothing contact, the totality of his body held, we produce a rubber thing to stick in his mouth and stimulate his sucking urge and fool him into forgetting what he really wants and needs. Imagine, ladies and gentlemen, how truly clever we are: that at this very early age we have the power to begin to robotize him, give him substitute warmth, substitute contact, a mother's arm-heart-breast-skin-touch wrapped up in a tiny twenty-five-cent rubber object. Fantastic bargain! Step up and get yours. Get two while you're at it so you can keep one sterilized at all times.

From this it's but a small jump to all those other substitutes— those other pacifiers that deprive us of an alive contact with the real human thing, the real human feeling, the real human up, the real human down, the flow, the spark, the real human electricity undrugged, unworded, unstereotyped, unsafe—risky—spontaneous —alive.

Take your choice—find your contact with your reality or get a substitute up with a joint (of the beer and/or reefer variety).

In America, since the Marilyn Monroe era, the breasts have become the big sex symbol, replacing the nether parts, being used for show and not for function. And with the growth of the breasts as a sex symbol, their real biological function has become submerged, suppressed, denied, condemned.

I once had a pediatrician in New York—one of those guys who have a big reputation, an office full of cattle people, and an iron-clad connection with one of New York's best hospitals. It was my first baby and I was as stupid as most other new mothers in our culture, except that I knew that I wanted to nurse my baby. This "doctor" put me and my baby on a rigid four-hour schedule, which didn't work out well at all. When I complained to him that my baby was crying before the four hours were up and that I thought maybe I should nurse him more frequently, he looked at me with a dire gaze and declaimed that if I nursed my baby more than every four hours "you would be using your breast as a pacifier!" Horrors, I thought. I was already prejudiced against pacifiers and the doctor's threatening tones made it seem as though I'd be committing a terrible wrong. And I must admit my frailty . . . I was overwhelmed by the threat implied in his tone of voice. It wasn't until considerable time had passed that I was able to break away from this mechanized, vegetabilized, and vegetabilizing "doctor" who had such contempt for the most natural biological function that exists between a mother and her infant.

These experts again!—let us beware of them. They will first vegetabilize us and then lead us into the sterilized vacuum-packed uniform-size can. And when we are canned, in neat little rows (remember the ticky-tacky houses?), we can then help in the process by producing more cans, cannier cans, bottled kids, the frozenest kids in the whole damn world.

Back to the infant, the Buddhist . . . growing, beginning to separate himself from his mother's breast, from his surrounding world . . . beginning to look at his hand and feel its separation from his eye . . . beginning to make some fantastic electrical connections in his brain . . . beginning through these connections, which took millions of years to evolve, to have some control over that hand and its movements . . . reaching out toward a bright object . . . reaching . . . brain-eye-hand in some discordant, dysynchronized, primitive dance reaching . . . reaching . . . overreaching . . . crying . . . angered . . . reaching . . . almost . . . almost . . . nearer . . . almost . . . *yes* . . . *success* . . . *mastery* . . . *I* have *it* . . . I, who have been helpless, without control, disconnected and yet without separation from all that surrounds me . . . at one amorphous oneness with the Universe . . . have been separating myself out and taking form . . . have been becoming . . . becoming an identity . . . becoming connected . . . and my hands are exploring and discovering that separated universe . . . are attempting to control the *it* around the *me* . . . to master all the *it*s and even all the *them*s. My lack of control and lack of mastery anger me and I try harder . . . and harder . . . and I don't give up . . . over and over again . . . I yell, scream, kick, cry, and keep trying . . . all the time I keep trying . . . to

133

achieve . . . to overcome . . . to overcome my frustration . . . to succeed where I have failed.

Here, now, I reach . . . again . . . again . . . but: Oh, death! —what is happening—as I reach now, at my first utterance of frustration—at my nearest cry—I receive the object thrust into my hands. A "helpful" parent or grandparent has just set a mold—my *cry*—not my reaching—not my mastery—brings the rattle, the ball, the person. I am truly magic. *I don't have to reach. I just cry.*

And here, in these earliest days, I learn to push the button—a cry pushes your "helpfulness" button—my arms need not reach out. Later I will seek to fold my atrophied arms around myself and order others to push the buttons and I won't even have to cry . . . in fact, I will lose touch ·with my tears and forget how to cry altogether. At this earliest age you, you helpers, you kind indulgent souls, have robbed me of achievement—of my ability to joy in reaching out, struggling with, and overcoming. You have robbed me of the greatest achievement of all—my very Life Force, my animality forcing its mastery over my universe—you have robbed me of my joy . . . that overwhelming thrill when I have, after my very own angry struggles, achieved my object, my goal.

Don't you see that the ball or rattle are meaningless to me—that the material object is *nothing*—that I, my achievement, my struggle, my mastery are *all!* What is this ball that you thrust into my hands—what has it to do with reaching-life-force-animal-nature, challenge, battle, aggression, and oh—beautiful, joyful overcoming . . . coming over . . . I have with my own efforts made this come over to me by overcoming it . . . I am . . . and I am all . . . now that I have achieved this ball, this rattle. Oh, you thief— you death dealer—forever after I shall think I am reaching for bright-colored objects . . . for balls and rattles and other material things . . . *and forget that it is my reaching alone that is all there really is.* And I shall weaken before my material universe . . . shall weaken before I have had the feel of strengthening.

Oh, darkness, descending on those infants "trailing clouds of glory." The first step to assure his helplessness and his weakness, the first step to imprison the man or woman within the infant . . . has just been achieved. From this early imprisoning, the vegetative steps that follow are easy. Vegetables "do not move out to get their nutrition."

And before we leave that maimed infant with his helplessness engraved forever upon him . . . with his phenomenal human-animal brain connections severed, flapping aimless in disconnected strands . . . let us turn to the maimer—the en-graver—the, if you will, parent. Oh, "helpful" one—who is it you are really trying to help—who is really the object of your indulgence? When you stop your infant's cry by giving him the object, or worse, sticking in a pacifier—like a dry fuck—the earliest tranquilizer killer of all—cheating him of his right to cry . . . whom are you really doing it all for? Come now, face up to the feelings of helplessness engendered in *you* when the baby cries—the intolerable feeling of frustration and maybe even defeat that *you* experience—the rage that may even be murderous and accounts for the so-called "battered child syndrome" . . . and then answer the question: Whom are you trying to help when you stifle your baby's cry . . . his life cry? If you can answer this question honestly, facing the frustration and anger in yourself when your kid cries, great!—there's hope for you and your kid to really make it in a loving, growth-stimulating relationship. That's the paradox—saying hello to your anger-hate feelings allows you also to embrace your tender-loving feelings, both being expressions of the human animal in his present stage of evolution.

Sometimes this murderous rage in the parent flows over . . . and instead of his crippling his little kid in slow degrees as is more usual, he kills him outright. In America, *every day,* at least one pre-school kid is killed by his own parents. There is even a parents' group, similar to Alcoholics Anonymous, called MOM, of parents who have trouble controlling their impulses to murder their children. This is the other extreme of the vegetable—man gone berserk, losing his connections with his loving feelings altogether.

What a sad state if the only two alternatives were these extremes:

pacifying and stifling the kid's healthy growing or erupting into uncontrolled rage and murdering the kid. But there is a world between these extremes . . . can you find that world? . . . can you let him cry . . . let him struggle . . . let him feel frustration and let him feel himself overcoming . . . let him feel *his* strength, not just yours, *his* mastery, not just yours, *his* rage, not your stifled-stifling shout turned into being-nice-to-baby with the rage buried then in a silent, conspiratorial pact between the two of you forever. If you gotta use a pacifier, damnit, put it in your own mouth, and let him go—and grow.

All right—we enter phase 2—or 22—or a million and 22. The child is past infancy—early school age. The parents are going for a drive or a trip or what-have-you. He, the child, is sitting in the back of the car (it's the safest place for him—actually standing behind the driver's seat is—but that's beside the point). The parents are talking—about taxes, or furniture, or Aunt Mary. That too is irrelevant. What *is* relevant is that the third person of the trio is not being talked to, is not being listened to, is hushed or reprimanded when he interrupts the conversation. If and when he really gets insistent, the parents may tolerate an impatiently heard sentence or two and then go on with their conversation as if pausing to brush away a fly.

What would you feel if you were that third person—what do you feel when you *are* that third person, that nuisance of a fly? We can pay attention—attend to—only one person at a time. When I, as a parent, am talking to my spouse, I cannot attend to you back there. In the car you get the back of my head—or the back of my hand if you try to interrupt too much.

So much for the third party—the third-class citizen—a league below those second-class citizens in our American culture: blacks and women, who also aren't listened to by our deaf and dumb majority. So here we have the confusing situation of the kid being catapulted from one extreme (parents responding to the infant's barest whimper) to the other (parents tuning his words out altogether).

Get in touch with your own feelings as you experience a denial of your presence . . . the helplessness . . . the futile feelings engendered in you by this . . . the inability to "get in" . . . the blankness and drifting off when you are not being fed by someone's attention . . . the turning off . . . and you begin to come close to what a child experiences who is made nonexistent. Many children go through their entire childhood this way. (As I've said, blacks and women frequently experience this when, because of their color or sex, they are "wiped out" of existence, made invisible as in Ralph Ellison's *Invisible Man*.)

Let us now consider the child learning to tie his shoelace, slipping the end in a loop, the rabbit's ear, instead of around it, pulling the end through . . . hopeful . . . and then impatient and frustrated at the failure of the lace to form a bow. The awkward fingers and thumbs pushing, pulling the lace—the fantastic concentration . . . the energy leaping along all those fine nervous connections to result in repeated failures and frustrations . . . until, one day . . . one miraculous bright day . . . with a yell of triumph . . . he has succeeded! . . . the bow is achieved! . . . the goal reached! The thrill . . . the glow of achievement is his—his very own. This is his victory.

This heightened sensation of joy occurs only when the child has tried to achieve . . . has used his own efforts . . . his own power. If, however, his "helpful" parents keep tying his shoelace for him long after his brain's connections have been made but not turned on by doing, by experiencing, then the response of the child when he finally does, postmaturely, tie his own bow is a dull response indeed —dull like the seeping out of semen from a partly flaccid, non-orgastic penis long after the excitement has been deadened and gone.

The excitement of achievement in the conquering of the shoelace —what happens to it after the first blush of victory becomes an everyday occurrence, when the battle of the brain's connections need no longer be fought, when the tying of the lace can take place in the dark, without effort . . . without eyes . . . without attention? The excitement becomes deadened with habit. Never again

137

will the thrill of tying a shoelace take on the same magnificence. Other battles must be sought and fought . . . other achievements struggled for . . . the button in the buttonhole, the pencil lettering words on a paper . . . never-ending, more and more and more to struggle with and to overcome. Life—to struggle with and experience.

And it is this very struggle for which there can be no blueprint. The opposite extreme of no help at all is equally damaging when the child is looking for *needed* attention and encouragement. If he needs help in a school subject, for example, the tuned-in parent knows when to coach him, when to support him, intervene with a teacher or principal, get him a tutor. Yes . . . inattention when a child is needing it for growth is as deadening as is the crippling super-helpfulness.

. My main point is—life has no easy formulas and much good is accomplished by the parent's being more open to the vibrations of growth going on in his child and less open to social pressures of conformity. Parents selecting clothes for the growing child that please the parents' sense of social propriety and that displease the child, insisting on "appropriate" hair styles (appropriate for parental and not child's taste), are blinding themselves to the urges of individuality and self-expression necessary for their child's ultimate independence.

About attention, I'm reminded of a ten-year-old boy, Bruce, who said he had a problem in getting attention from his father and wanted me to help him. He described his father as coming home from work, eating his dinner, joking around during dinner, and then plunking down before the TV until bedtime. Whenever Bruce approached him with a question or statement, his father continued to watch TV while muttering some perfunctory remarks. He had never taken his son out with him alone and there were no exclusive father-son activities that Bruce could ever recall. Also, the only time the son got any contact with his father was when he would sit or lie next to him while his father watched TV, and his father would run his hands through Bruce's hair and haphazardly caress Bruce's

138

body. The father later cited this as evidence that he gave Bruce lots of "attention."

I decided we could not solve the problem without the father's participation in the session and the father agreed to come in with his son. Early in the session, with Bruce and his father sitting face to face, I asked the father to listen to Bruce's statement of his problem. A few sentences were barely out of Bruce's mouth when the father got defensive and began "explaining" and excusing himself with many rationalizations that came out like subtle counterattacks. I interrupted him, told him there was no need for him to defend himself, that no one was judging him, and that all I wished him to do was to listen to Bruce so he could understand Bruce's view of his own problem. There then occurred a minor miracle—this heavily defended father, when told not to talk but just to listen, actually began to *listen* to his son's pain, frustration, desire for contact, and for a sign of his father's love. The tears began to flow from the eyes of both father and son (and from my own), and the father said he had never realized Bruce felt this way. By the end of the session the father expressed eagerness to do some father-son things with Bruce. I was moved by the amount of real contact and flow between them. I pointed out gently, not discussing any homosexual formulations but simply the growing-up process, that Bruce was getting too old for his father to caress him and play with his hair, and that the plans they were making to do things together and to have times of private real talk similar to what they were doing in my office were much more valuable to Bruce and to his father and they both agreed. At the end of the session there was a sense of elation and hopefulness, a realization of their mutual love, and a confidence that they had built a most necessary bridge to the new journey they were planning together.

No . . . there is no blueprint for the kind of attention the kid needs. Tuning-in, listening to the kid, is the best way I know of coming close to understanding what his needs really are.

From the sensitive soil of a child's brain there is indeed no blueprint to tell us at the moment into what strange forms our unwitting seeds of words and behavior will later grow. Paul, at twenty-three, came into treatment drugged out of his skull with LSD, hash, mescaline, and hosts of other drugs. After a few months he gave up the drug trip and took to caring for himself and his body. He continued in treatment, and for several weeks he told me he was withholding a "terrible" secret from me of which he was ashamed. Finally, in one session, he decided to confess. After much to-do and hemming and hawing, Paul finally said he had moles or freckles on his back and he was ashamed of them and kept them covered all the time. (So much for my speculations as to the nature of his shameful secret!) He related the onset of his shame to an incident that occurred when he was around ten years old. He was visiting his grandmother and was wearing a bathing suit and "she asked me what are those brown spots on your back . . . or something like that."

E: All right. Be your grandmother right now and let her say the things that she didn't say to you that were on her mind when she said that.

P: Just say it, like I think her head was saying it?

E: Yes, let her call you by name, by whatever name she used.

P: Uh—OK—uh—(long delay, breathing heavily) Paul, uh, what are those brown spots on your back—uh, they're really ugly.

E: Now, look at her and respond to her.

P: Uh . . . how do you want . . . what do you mean? Respond to her like I responded?

E: No—the way you really feel right now.

P: What I would say?

E: Yes, she's saying this to you . . . how old are you then?

P: Maybe eight or so . . . maybe I am older, ten or twelve.

E: What do you think of her saying that to you? What do you feel?

P: Well, it's pretty crushing.

E: Yes—tell her.

P: Tell her what?

E: Tell her that.

P: Right now?

140

E: Right now, tell her.

P: (Meekly, apologetically) That's a pretty crushing thing to say to your grandson.

E: That's right. (Pause) Now say something crushing back. So you can get her off your back. She's on your back.

P: Uh huh.

E: It's not just the spots on your back, it's your grandmother on your back, too. And the only way to get her off your back is to say something crushing back to her, right now. (Long pause)

P: Just say . . . lash out, huh?

E: Yes, go ahead.

P: (Mildly, gently, softly) Get off my back, you fat old thing.

E: Louder.

P: (Still gentle) Get off my back, you fat old thing.

E: You're holding it in, Paul—get it out.

P: Louder?

E: She's not gonna get off your back with a little tiny voice like that.

P: Yeah. Well—yeah.

E: You gotta get that big fat old thing off your back—it needs a big voice, a big fat old voice to do it.

P: (More lively, but still gentle) Get off my back, you fat old thing.

E: More!

P: Get off my back, you fat old thing.

E: Look, just bend over and I'll get on your back. I'm your grandmother—OK? (I put as much weight as possible, leaning my torso full over his back.)

P: And you want me to?

E: (Loudly) Yes, go ahead—yell it out.

P: (Vigorously) Get off my back, you fat old thing.

E: Louder.

P: Get off my back—get off my back, goddamnit!

E: (Yelling) I can't hear you.

P: Get off my back, you fat old thing.

E: I can't hear you. You're just an ugly boy with ugly spots on your back.

P: Get off my back!

E: I can't hear a word you're saying . . . you're just an ugly boy.

P: (Angry now) Get off my back, ya fat shit!

E: Make me—you can't make me—I'm on your back and I'm gonna stay here forever. (For the first time he struggles to remove my 125-pound weight off his back, I struggle to stay on, his struggle increases, and finally he shoves me off. We are breathless for a while with the effort.) What are you feeling right now?

P: I'm not sure. (Sighs)

E: You've been carrying that woman on your back. It's not the brown spots on your back that bug you, it's that fat old thing that you've been carrying on your back for over a dozen years. That's a heavy weight. It would have been very easy for me to recommend that you get those taken off—it's a very simple thing—the doctor goes swish, swish, and they're off. But that would've been terrible to do that and still have the fat old woman on your back. You gotta get her off your back first, and then if you choose to get rid of those things you can get rid of them—or maybe they're not so important and you can leave them. But you can't get rid of them until you get rid of her first, because she's the fat old thing on your back.

P: (Sighs deeply)

E: Do that again, Paul. (He breathes deeply several times.) What are you feeling right now?

P: (Pause) Well, I feel a little more at ease. I feel the blood rushing to my head, which makes me feel good, ya know . . . and uh—well, I kinda feel good that I told you about it, ya know.

E: Paul, there was one point there where instead of repeating the same thing: "get off my back, ya fat old thing" you suddenly said: "You shit!"—like you were *really* getting into it . . . and then you pulled back from that and then you stayed with just repeating.

P: Yeah—

E: What pulled you back from that?

142

P: Uh—well, you know, I have very fond feelings for my grand-parents, you know.

E: Listen, that doesn't mean you can't have negative feelings too.

P: Yeah—and—ya know, my grandfather just died and my grandmother's so sensitive right now, ya know.

E: She wasn't so sensitive when she told you that you have ugly things growing on your back. She was telling you you're ugly and what little kid likes to hear he's ugly?

P: Yeah . . . so I don't know.

E: Listen, is it hurting her that you said get off my back, you fat old thing, you shit—you called her a shit.

P: (Laughs)

E: (Louder) You called her a shit!

P: (Laughs more)

E: Is it hurting her . . . did she drop dead because you said that—in here?

P: That I . . . because I . . .

E: Yes, is she still living out there?

P: Yeah.

E: You didn't kill her by calling her a shit in here.

P: Uh uh.

E: Or calling her a fat ugly old thing . . . or telling her to get off your back.

P: Yeah—yeah, I feel better now.

At the end of this session Paul left behind a weight he had carried for over a dozen years. What will become of his spots (actually not at all bad looking) remains to be seen.

Let's go to another phase. When the child, who has never had the experience in his family of being listened to, reaches adolescence and begins to leave the family surveillance and establish independent, separate relationships, he experiences *for the first time in his life* that someone, namely his peer, is listening to him! (Remember that scene in Romain Rolland's *Jean Christophe* when, for the first time in his isolated life, Jean finds a friend and runs all the way home from school shouting over and over again: "I have a friend,

I have a friend!"—over and over again in excited breathlessness.)

What a feeling this gives—to be listened to, to be heard! Someone really cares what I say—(not the kind of "caring"—caring for whom, again?—that criticizes my grammar or my foul language). And I want to listen—and I do—I do listen to my peers as they listen to me. And we listen to one another. And this is the answer when my mother asks: "Why do you listen to those bums?" Answer: "They listen to me."

So, if the price I have to pay for being in with my listeners is doing what they do—taking the pot and other drugs they do—well, man, it's a small price to pay for that fantastic feeling of being listened to! Besides, I *want* to do what they do, I want to be like them—they *listen* to me!

What can we do to stop perpetuating generations of vegetables, of vegetabilized children?

One fantastic antidote to the deadening of a child lies in searching out the child in ourselves and letting it breathe and come out.

Beneath many of the uptight, struggling, tormented grown-ups I contact, I see the laughing, fighting, loving, cruelly hating child pushed out of sight. When I address myself not to the parent figure in front of me, but to the hiding child in the patient, respecting his (the child's) feelings, the grown-up begins to open the door, embarrassedly at first, and let him tentatively come out.

I saw a man in his late fifties who was a very successful businessman and a very unsuccessful father. He came from out of town for a consultation regarding his son, an eighteen-year-old young man. The father had the usual complaints of his son's being on drugs, a school dropout, and above all he complained of lack of communication with his son. The father, a big, obese man, stiff and proper and affluent, with held-in breath, somehow gave me the feeling that he was dying. I told him he had the look of a corpse, whereupon he told me how he was killing himself, how he always pushed himself in business and "couldn't" stop. He never let up pressuring himself to do more and more. He had already had one heart attack and this still didn't stop him. He felt that he wouldn't make it past sixty.

How to deal with a dying man who was planning his death in less than ten years? I asked him to project the time forward to the time of his death, and together we planned for his funeral and went through the burial scene. As he fantasized lying in his coffin, I asked him to look at the faces and reactions of each of the surrounding mourners, and then to feel the dirt being shoveled on top of him in his coffin. During this process, he seemed to come in touch with his dying and then became impatient and somewhat resentful of the tyrannical parent part of himself driving him. I then began to encourage him to allow his child out. Believe it or not, that very proper, highly educated and intelligent, huge, most properly dressed man allowed himself the joy of prancing around my office with a lampshade on his head . . . and it was his own idea to do this . . . his own creative "fuck you" to the death-dealing uptight parent figure breathing down his neck. For a moment he experienced a carefree joy, a letting go, and a freely breathing beingness, maybe for the first time in his adult life.

When he left my office, he left behind a ton of his weight—his burdened weight. I'm certain that when next he saw his son (he was returning home the following day) he listened and spoke to him with a different air . . . hopefully with the air, not of a business tycoon, but of a man wearing a lampshade on his balding head.

Parents' crippling of the child is often aided by professionals who write the how-to books. Those psychologizing books on "understanding your child" make me sick . . . if parents swallowed these whole hog they'd make their children even sicker.

"Now darling, I know you didn't really mean to hit Johnny—he's your friend—you love him—let's discuss what was *really* going on, dear." Or, "Now, dear, I know you feel upset just now—let's talk about it—let's sit down together and find out what's wrong." Ugh!

The crappiest thing you can do to your kid is to explain away every tinge of forbidden, undesirable feeling according to your gospel of life. The kids I see who have been psyched out of their gut feelings by these kinds of psychology-book-reading-progressive-understanding parents are really in bad shape, mostly guilt-ridden,

145

crushed, and stifled personalities who no longer know what they "really feel" about anything . . . blank and vegetablelike.

In addition to stifling the emotional flow, there is no stifling of the intellect so severe as occurs when the parent *always* has an explanation for *everything*—all doubts are patly put to rest, every question has a ready-made answer . . . there is no room for a doubt or question to breathe (let alone whisper), to remain unanswered. It's like imposing the ruling absolutism of a God-tyrant-führer or what-have-you on that fabulous questioning-searching-wishing-hoping-miracle-making wonderment that is a child's mind.

The child is the discoverer of the unchartered course that finds new continents, new galaxies. When the "helpful," knowledgeable parent binds the child's mind with his own hand-me-down charter, he cuts that magnitudinous, infinitely reaching mind down to the size of his own procrustean mentality and thus buries forever all in his child that goes beyond himself . . . he kills the far reaches of the child's mind and introduces a static process of dull, unimaginative repetition and therefore of decay.

You want to give your kid your biases? OK! Be strong, if you are, about them? OK!—but at least tell the kid it's your *belief,* your *faith,* your *suspicion,* your *superstition.* Don't pass these on as factual validatable realities . . . tell him other people exist with *other* beliefs (or lack of them), other faiths (or lack of them), other suspicions and superstitions . . . and they think they're as right about theirs as you think you are about yours. And level with him—tell him it's *easier for you* if he accepts your faith, not because it's the "only true faith," but because it makes it *easier for you* if he accepts uniformity and conformity with you. The shit about its being for *his* benefit reeks—don't drown him and yourself in it. At least level the usual destructive hypocrisy . . . level with your kid . . . and get straight about your own motives. It will take the stench of decay out of your relationship with him, keep him straight in his relationship with you and himself, and allow his mind and his guts to freely find their own way through this "vale of tears" and joy.

146

Crippling the Kid or Early Makings of a Vegetable

And it will give him the chance to tell you, straight, that he's not in this life to make things *easier* for you or for him. It will give him the chance to get straight and unconfused in the mess of hypocritical confusions surrounding us. And with both of you getting your heads straight, there may be a chance for a head-on collision that might lead to a gut-on collision, which might be a beautiful encounter with your kid, an enlightening hating-loving-yielding-sharing real experience.

Take a chance—get real with yourself, your doubts (you can't be real without these) . . . let your kid feel the reality of your doubts—tell him—share—this is *real* loving and caring and giving and growing.

Wild Wonder

They say the sky and air are free,
The rain, the sea, the thunder.
But these remain apart, if we
Should lose our wild wonder.
These can't be had at any cost
With our dear wild wonder lost.

Then let me look out on the world
The way a child sees it.
And leave no curling leaf unfurled,
No cat dead but I'll grieve it.

I'll pay the cost of any pain
To have my wonder back again.

7

GROUPISM
VERSUS
THE PERSON

The whole thing about being a healthy human animal in America
boils down to this: Can I be civilized and still be my own animal
person? Can I be my own animal person while my civilization
demands that I be categorized as a member of a group (family,
political, professional, religious, racial, gender, national, etc.)?
Do groups exist to which I can belong and still be an individual,
or are those terms "group" and "individual" an absolute contradiction?

Let's start with the group of two called the marriage couple. When
I am an individual and you are an individual, I can merge with you,
respect your differences and my own, and emerge again. In vain
I give myself to you, for I am returned to endless give again. If,
though, I give up all my own boundaries to follow you, to please
you, to become you, I lose myself. When I lose myself, you lose me
and I lose you. Then I get angry. But at whom? Who is there to
get angry at . . . oh, it's all so confusing . . . I confuse myself
with you . . . and I never emerge whole again.

So .˙. . stay near me . . . but be sure to go away too . . . and I will do the same. There is part of me you can never know . . . part of you I can never know . . . I blend my mystery with yours and *I don't have to know it all* . . . *I don't have to tell it all*. We can respect each other's essential mystery . . . let us stay with our surmises and surprises and wonderments. Let us stay and go . . . know and not know . . . know and wonder. Our mysteries unite.

When two people give up their individualities altogether upon entering a relationship, disaster falls. Let's look at it this way:

Each person, alone, has a charge; let us say that the female (♀) has a positive charge and the male (♂) has a negative one. There is an attraction in the opposite charges; they are drawn together, come closer. The closer they come, the more strongly charged is the situation until they unite, let us say, in the sexual embrace. At this point the opposite charges reach their climax of intensity, and at the moment of total union there is simultaneous discharge. When the positive and the negative forces unite, there is a canceling out of the charges, which become zero.

So, if I remain united with you, I lose my charge, you lose yours, and we are two zeros united.

Can you imagine how this phenomenon operates in marriages where each partner gradually gives up the charge of all outside interests, submerges the individual separate entity, and becomes a zero, and thus contributes zero charge to the relationship!

I had a patient who, during twenty years of marriage never— not once—outside of going to work, did anything *alone*—never did anything without his wife. Never dared, even, to venture out to a movie he wanted to see if his wife didn't want to go. Gradually, he gave up all his individual interests, convinced himself that he really didn't like to go to movies by himself (he used to love westerns, which his wife abhorred, and he went grudgingly to art films that he at best tolerated) until he finally found it impossible to even conceive of going to a movie alone without great anxiety. Important? Well, maybe the movie issue is not all that critical, there aren't that many good westerns, but he paid for this type of adjustment by crippling himself and his sexual apparatus as well. Finally, having emasculated himself, having given his balls away and turned himself into an impotent zero, he began getting paranoid about his wife's having a lover with functioning balls.

Wow! How many times is this pattern repeated in the marriages around you . . . or your own? How many marriages do you know where the two people have their electrical charges, where they really listen to each other, look at each other? Go into any restaurant and look at how married couples look at each other. Rarely do you see an alive relationship. Rarely do you have a sense of their discovering each other. If there is nothing more to discover . . . if the pattern is known, memorized, rehearsed, anticipated, turned off . . . the marriage is a dead zero.

The solution? Keep sufficiently apart to the point of feeling— this I have of me which is only mine, which is unrelated to anyone else in the world. When there is truly part of me that is mine, for me, there is then part of me left over to give to you. I renew my charge from that undischarged part of me that is only mine.

When no part of me is my own, I become your appendage. I then can give you nothing, since I am already part of you. I then depend on you for my motive force, for my charge; since you give me only your own charge, my charge is the same sign as yours, and we have then no attraction between us, no electrical current.

So stay apart—and I will stay apart. I will nourish my differences and support yours. I will keep my charges charged—come to you, merge with you, discharge, and become zero . . . and remove myself and become charged again . . . and, so charged, pursue our common interests and contribute a greater charge to these. I will resist the inertia of remaining inert. I will jealously guard my charges. I will explode in the unity of becoming inert and fly off again to rediscover my electricity. I will ebb and flow with you . . . I will be the storm and the calm with you . . . we will be forever changing and thence forever alive with each other.

A thirty-year-old woman with marital problems (husband excessively jealous, she is not responsive to him, thinks him ugly, and claims nonetheless to love him) tells me: "My ego is boosted by people thinking well of me." As we explore this, it turns out that her "ego" depends on other people's opinion; her behavior and feelings are always geared to the other person's approval. She keeps her figure slim to please other people. I ask her: "Whom are your sexual and sensual feelings for?"

And do you know—she is stunned, unable to answer this question—totally blocked. She is a woman so used to using her brain to lie to her body, saying a pseudo-yes with her body while her innards are repelled by having sex, and, conversely, seeming aloof and cold when her impulses are urging her to the sexual embrace.

I ask her to visualize being turned on by her husband and she says: "Oh, I can't do that." So, undaunted, I tell her to pretend to do it, and she blithely goes over the barrier, gets into a sex scene with her husband, and goes on to visualize having intense sexual and sensual feelings and finally orgasm. After this, we talk about the sexual feelings she had in her fantasy and she says they felt real and very exciting. Now again, I ask her: "Whom are those sexual feelings for?" And she says spontaneously: "Myself—they're for me— I don't give them away when I experience them. They're mine." The following evening, for the first time in years, she experienced an orgasm during intercourse with her husband. Weeks later she told me that the best thing I had given her so far in the few months of her therapy was the notion that her sexual feelings were all hers, that by having sexual relations she does not give away her sexual feelings: "They're all mine—they're always mine—I *can't* give them away!" she exulted.

Now, let's talk about this honesty shit in the marriage group. If a guy or gal wants to screw someone not his wife (or husband) that's one thing; when he does it, that's another thing; when he comes back and tells his spouse, that's still another thing. I've never seen this type of "honesty" in a marriage where it wasn't used somehow sadistically or as a whip of some kind to hold over the marital partner. What is hidden beneath the honesty is the true motive: the sadistic thrust, the cruel put-down, the defense against homosexuality, the dumping of guilt. The marriage partner is not a confessional receptacle. Go to church if you need one, or to a boozin' buddy, or find a stranger, or a psychiatrist who'll listen, and don't dump your guilt on your partner!

When an infant has hunger pangs it cries immediately . . . if it has a peristaltic rush, it craps in its diapers . . . if the peristalsis is in reverse, it vomits. It has little or no control over what comes out of its mouth or asshole. It's as though both orifices are perpetually open. But when I get past infancy, I learn to control these openings —with my mouth, I can decide what to put into it and what to let out of it. I don't have to eat it all . . . I don't have to tell it all. With my anus I have some control over when to let things out of it and, of course, what to let into it. (I have had women patients tell me that their husbands demanded anal intercourse with them, frequently describing men with short staying powers or other erectile problems. These women have on occasion allowed this, often not enjoying it or even being repelled by the anal approach but feeling there was "something wrong" with them for not liking it. They had not learned that they are entitled to their tastes, entitled to say no, entitled to control what goes into their orifices. I'm not referring here to the women who like this approach.)

Telling someone "the whole truth" without control may be like shitting on them with your mouth: Do I tell you the truth because "I can't lie"—"I just can't control myself—I just can't stand to lie?" —bullshit! Take some paregoric before you vomit your "truth" all over me!

Listen—this is not to say that there are not some couples who can openly share marital infidelities with each other without disturbing their relationship—it's just that I have never met them in my practice. I've treated some wild swingers who gave lip service to sharing their sexual partners with others, but when the chips were down, brother!—the same conventional moralizing, sugarcoated and disguised though it was, emerged in bitterness.

In fact, couples who are swingers (spouse swappers), and the entire society of swingers for that matter, operate on a rigid rule of

153

sex *without* emotional involvement. The sex is mechanically free and open—like opening a door on oiled hinges. The emotions are tight, enclosed, buried, and considered to be threatening and are thus verboten. "Screw him," says the husband, "but make sure you don't feel any *emotional* involvement with him or it's quits." The wife gives her husband the same ultimatum. (I wonder if this taboo on feeling flow is a cleverly built-in rationalization for their having wooden feelings to begin with?)

Telling everything is *not* honesty—it's the worst form of hiding. With swingers, whose ethical rules of behavior include an injunction against feelingful involvement, what is hidden is the despair at the lack of ability to become involved emotionally. Their behavior is all a mouth-cunt-cock-anus-earhole trip—mechanical, agitated emotionlessness, with no heart or belly or passion involved—no flow—no heat—no beat.

Hey! In your swinging marriages, if you have to expose something to each other, why not expose the deadness beneath this frenzied searching activity. If you contact the deadness and maybe the concern about homosexuality and share them, you have at least some honest chance of a resurrection!

Now let's go on to the family group. Many parents act as though each individual in the family is part of an organic whole . . . get that? . . . a *part* of a whole. So the family members can fight as though they are individuals when their doors are closed, but to the outside world they are supposed to present a united front (the neighbors might hear!) . . . political parties, medical and other authoritarian groups, nations, and all other varieties of clubs do the same. (Judges and lawyers belong to the same club . . . your doctor and the AMA belong to the same club . . . so where can John Doe go to redress a wrong done him by a club member? The answer is clear—he can go only to another club member, and he's never likely to get redress.)

If you threaten your family group by becoming an individual . . . no longer a "part" but rather individually apart . . . then they act

154

as though you're threatening to dissolve the cement of the entire group.

A father of a twenty-eight-year-old Jewish woman told me that if his daughter went with a non-Jewish man he would disinherit her; if she married a black man he would rather see her dead. "How could she think of doing such a thing *to me!*" This father does not see his daughter as a person and thereby depersonalizes not only her but himself . . . the master becoming the slave to his slave . . . dependent on his slave's actions, wholly enwrapped by them, fixated on them . . . imprisoned. Ironically, while he was venting his tirades, his daughter (a blond, blue-eyed, fair-skinned social worker) was indeed having an affair with a very black black man, a psychologist. Still more ironically, she ultimately married a Jewish man around forty years of age, a clerk in a department store, and still the father objected. Well—you can't win them all; in this instance, you can't win *at all*.

How can I, as parent, guide my child to grow into his individuality while still encouraging his participation in his peer group so that he isn't the oddball outsider? First, my duty as a parent is *not* to make my child comfortable (conformity to the group is comforting, tranquilizing—the greatest nonmedical but nonetheless physiological tranquilizer of all . . . even more so than television) . . . *no!* my duty is to make my child *not* comfortable but rather alive. So when my daughter in Miami and, a few years earlier, my son in Beverly Hills came home from kindergarten and asked for a nickel to bring to school for a Red Cross contribution, I explained that I don't contribute to the Red Cross . . . I tried as best I could to let my five-year-old children know some five-year-old explanation of the facts that during World War II the Red Cross actually *separated* "white" blood from "black" blood . . . also they have no black people among their high-salaried administrators. Now . . . more than my tiny and insignificant five-cent protest against the Red Cross, I was teaching my children that the pressure of group conformity (get your Red Cross buttons, children!) . . . the pres-

155

sure from teachers and others in authority as well as peer pressure
. . . can be questioned and disapproved of. Of course, it's uncomfortable for a kid not to have a Red Cross button to stick on
a lapel when all the other kids have them. (I recall Browning's
poem about the turncoat Wordsworth in "The Lost Leader"—
"Just for a handful of silver he left us, Just for a riband to stick
in his coat . . .") Yes, it's even more distressing for my kid not
to have a lollipop while all the other kids are drooling over their
cavity producers. No, I won't let my kid eat anything containing
sugar or white flour, both devitaminized and demineralized and
poisoned with bleaching agent chemicals. And now you'll call me
a faddist, right? You, with a martini in one hand, a cigarette in
the other—your kid with a lollipop in one hand, a Coke in the
other . . . and, because you're a member of the in group and I'm
definitely way out, you call me a faddist.

I admit, it's distressing for my kid to be deprived of lollipops,
Cokes, and all the rest of the chozzerai, but goddamn it, what's
a parent for? Just some puppet of the outer established order helping to keep the blanket on?

"But every kid eats lollipops" . . . bullshit! "How can you
be so cruel to your kid?" More bullshit! When I am a puppet of
the outer establishment, what happens to my insides . . . to my
kid's insides? Ulcer holes; enlarged heart and high-blood pressure;
dentures instead of teeth; inflated, constipated, cancerous guts . . .
nothing on the inner side but shit, and flaky or balled stuff at that.
"Get your Red Cross buttons, children . . . get your lollipops
. . . take the sweet and easy way . . . the safe way . . . get
what the neighbor's kids get . . . no, get more, bigger-better-
grander things than your neighbor's kids . . . *com* . . . *pet* . . .
it . . . *ion* . . . *hurray* . . . bigger . . . better . . . Sting-
Ray bikes won't do anymore . . . get yourself a motor bike
. . . mechanize your bike riding . . . mechanize your legs . . .
mechanize your head and heart . . . and keep your guts so filled
with establishment-group-conformity shit that no peristaltic elec-

trical movement takes place . . . it's easy . . . just do as you're told . . . just stay in line . . . like everyone else.

Hey, don't get me wrong. I don't lecture my kids about these things. Right now, living with my seven-year-old daughter, we're too busy fighting-arguing-yelling-laughing-working-loving-kissing-hugging and just plain talking to each other to have time to go in for philosophizing. I'll leave that for the pedants. Of course, she and I don't *like* being angry at each other . . . we get no pleasure out of it . . . but the outbursts erupt as naturally and inevitably as lightning in an electrical storm, being as much and as little a part of our nature as the thundering storm. Individual eruptions like these would happen naturally in a group that allowed them to occur. Eruptions clear and clean the air, and a breathing group can then go on growing.

People just don't seem to be able to *appreciate differences*. My daughter's kindergarten teacher, a top-level public-school teacher at that, said—when I told her why I wouldn't contribute to the Red Cross: "Oh, that's all right, I'll give Merissa a button anyway." She was concerned about Merissa's feeling different from all the kids with the buttons. She wouldn't understand when I told her it would not be necessary to give my daughter a button. God-damn it! Why does everyone want to take the easy way out (out . . . get that? . . . *out* . . . out of this world, out of your guts, a dropout from nature herself) all the time? Why the hell do we deprive everyone, especially kids, of *challenge?*

On the other side of this counter-peer, individualistic coin is the history of a forty-year-old patient, Karl, who had had some allergic respiratory condition as a child and whose father treated him like an invalid, refusing to allow him to go out to play with the other children after school and absolutely forbidding him to play ball, insisting also that he be excused from school gymnastics of any kind. Karl's fears of his father and of dying from physical exertion were overridden by his urge to be like the other boys, and he would climb out of his bedroom window after school and sneak off to play ball. Not only did he not succumb, but he went on to win a prize for excelling in sports and got his picture in the newspaper. By being *disloyal* to his father's dictates, joining his peer group's activities, he probably saved his life, which was, under his father's direction, headed for that of chronic invalidism. Although he survived, he did, however, pay a price for his guilt-ridden disloyalty. Thus, when I saw him, at age forty, he felt "blah," his spontaneity was totally submerged, his eyes and emotional expression were dulled, and the only time he felt a surge of aliveness was on the tennis court.

What kids today seem to be saying to their families is: I owe you no blind loyalty by the accident of my being born into your group. You must show me qualities worthy of respect before I respect you. The time of "Do as I say because I'm your parent, your teacher, your preacher, your country" is ending. Youth are saying: "Earn my loyalty, my respect."

Professional schools and organizations, political groups, trade unions can be used for joint action toward progress . . . and also for corruption of that progress. My racist medical school almost annihilated me for showing outrage at their cruel extinction of two black medical students. The southern medical board almost exterminated me as a physician in their state because they were following some policy that told them certain ideas I espoused (Wilhelm Reich's) were bad and should be eliminated. And the doctor's club, perhaps the worst of these groups, is doing its contemptible thing on your flesh.

Once in Philadelphia in my student years in the forties, I attended a leftist party meeting to see what it was all about. I was (still am) very naïve about politics, and the speaker was hammering a point home that the Philadelphia *Record* (liberal Democratic newspaper) was more dangerous and did more harm to the working class than the Philadelphia *Inquirer* (Republican-supported newspaper). In the rare times I read newspapers . . . (I still don't read them much, if at all . . . do the journalists and advertisers really have more to offer me than the poets, the essayists, the novelists . . . and, after all, since the news is written to *sell,* what is the difference between the average journalist's copy and the advertiser's copy? . . . I get most of the news of the world through my personal town criers . . . word of mouth from friends and acquaintances and patients) . . . in those rare times of reading newspapers, I had come across views supporting strikes and union activities in the *Record* and never in the *Inquirer,* so I raised my hand and questioned the speaker on this point. He lightly . . . derisively? . . . brushed away my questions and thus brushed me and my unanswered questions out of that meeting and I never returned. What was the matter with that speaker . . . had he never heard of the Socratic method . . . of questioning . . . of dissent? If I cannot question . . . *if I cannot doubt my own dogma* . . . I cease to grow . . . and my group fails with me.

Religious groups are destructive when they place dogma over individual health and well-being, as for example their crime against woman, forbidding her to decide whether or not to maintain a pregnancy. Most religious groups are guilty of destructive separatisms fostering animosities between in-group adherents and outsiders.

All separatism is not necessarily as stifling as is religious separatism. Blacks in America have gone through a militant separatist phase, probably the first big step toward appreciating their identity, their individuality. Militant women liberationists are now going through the same extreme phase . . . these separations provide a necessary step toward concepts of individual worth and paradoxically are necessary to ultimate integration on a more equal footing. Their separatism and dissent are essential not only to their growth but to the growth of American culture.

In America Black Panthers have been systematically murdered, revolutionaries of all kinds have been beaten and jailed . . . they have not been seen as individuals with dissent . . . (oh, how healthy is the voice of dissent . . . how we grow from it . . . how it nourishes us) . . . but rather as gangrenous parts we must cut off. The tragedy in families and nations is that we cut off individuals

159

as if they were disposable parts, and that is an unnatural crime. Individualists, dissenters, I hail you. I learn from you. You are my relentless mirror. If I am to live, I must nourish you and listen to you. I must not confuse you, Dissenters, with the destructive parts of myself you show me. So, risk your dissensions, your dreams and visions . . . I love you . . . your vitality . . . your electricity . . . your risks . . . your differences . . . how I love your differences. I am so fatigued by machine-made samenesses . . . I love your flaws . . . I lovingly caress each tiny human flaw of you . . . I even forgive you your polemicizing, your bullshitting, your infantilisms. Stay with your differences—therein you offer life to us all.

Any group that wipes out dissent is dangerous . . . tyrannical. The tyrannical group . . . a large maw that swallows you up as an individual and belches you forth as a homogeneous blend . . . an amorphous mass the particles of which are indistinguishable from one another. Goddamn dangerous! Imagine the "If you're not with us, you're against us" dictate of most groups . . . what a totality! Can't I be with some of your things and not with others? What's this all or none bit? I'm not an infant . . . do as I say or else! My maturity demands that you respect my judgment, my right to dissent, to follow when I wish and to go off alone in another direction when I wish. No wonder I rarely joined any groups, except compulsory ones like county medical societies when necessary or psychiatric groups that usually were not too relevant to anything except socializing . . . and curiosity as to who was doing what in the field. The New York County Medical Society, which I was compelled to join as a requisite to taking my boards in Psychiatry, later demanded that all members join the American Medical Association. I objected to this compulsory demand, wrote a letter of explanation to the society, and resigned.

But here's a puzzle for you! . . . how to remain an individual and still be part of a group action and interaction. It may be possible in encounter groups that focus on individual awareness, but even here if you have a dogmatic group leader who sets the group in a mold, you're stuck in position as long as you stay in the group.

Perhaps a group can be dangerous only if I give over my own judgment to it and let it dictate what I should think and feel.

What am I willing to give up in order to stay in a group? And what are you willing to give up for the group? That's the question we each have to answer for ourselves. Is being an American so important that I will go kill nonwhite babies, children, adults, and old people in Vietnam or any other place America's dogmatic self-interested group leaders dictate? This is the question for each person facing the draft . . . me, my dignity, my humanity . . . or follow the murdering group?

Destructiveness rendered by national groups knows no equal. World War I is a prime example of mass murder, followed by Germany's Nazi Deutschland uber Alles devastation and today's Vietnam horror.

I was granted a personal look beneath national separatisms on a trip I took to Europe in 1954, just after finishing my residency in psychiatry. It was my first expansive vacation. I saw the grandeurs in front and the alleyways in back (where typical tourists, staying in their groups, rarely tread). I saw the poverty hovels just outside the Vatican walls—just one block, mind you, from the Pope's palatial city . . . just a cat's call away from the Sistine Chapel and all that magnificence. And I won't forget the even more primitive hovels in the back-ways of Naples . . . yes, I admit, it is not only Washington, D.C., that has this ludicrous horror of wealth-poverty contrasts.

I returned from Europe with an impression of the markedly superficial differences between Americans and Europeans and also with a feeling of the essential samenesses of all peoples. The delicately balanced pH of the blood is the same the world over; underneath our skins and languages and customs our hearts beat with a like mechanism. We are all, despite our separation into myriad diverse groups, more alike than different.

What has my essential essence, my being, to do with the accident of my birthplace . . . what has breathing to do with the color of my skin . . . what has professional status, gender, or religion to do with snot or with peristalsis?

161

Yes, as for me—I am not particularly American or particularly white or particularly any one-group identified object. I am a person —international (between nations)—in a world of persons . . . in the future my group may become the universe or cosmos of persons.

What are you? . . . I'm a person.

What do you do? . . . I breathe.

rose of eight

rose, of eight, can yell:
"I hate your nose!"

at thirty, she may only smile
and no one will perceive the pose,
least of all

rose.

8

TO *BE* OR TO BE NICE: MOVEMENT, RISK, AND CONTACT

Rose . . . I see many Roses in my practice—nice ladies . . . out of contact with the not-so-nice little real girl within them. Is the little real child still alive in you . . . in me . . . or have we stifled the rose of her forever?

I want to tell you about risk-taking and I'm sitting here contacting what risks, if any, I took today. Actually, it was a safe day and no risk-taking until this evening when I drove up to one of those plush . . . almost palatial . . . new apartment houses on Collins Avenue in the fifties for a benefit dinner for A.N.'s Ballet Company. I waited in my battered old Volvo station wagon (which saw two cross-country trips, numerous camping trips up and down the mountains of New York and California, the fenders dented by New York trucks and autos mostly from merely being parked on New York City streets). I waited behind Cadillacs, Continentals, and Buicks for the attendant to park my car. The line was long and immobile, so I pulled out and drove up alongside of the first car that had been stationary for a long time, and, seeing the driver's simpàtico face

163

and not the stiff and veiled variety usually seen around this type of dwelling, I asked the face if he thought it would be okay for me to pull ahead and park it myself in the garage below and behind the building. He smiled at my "daring" (Jesus! Just think of the Panthers risking their lives daily for "the cause," and I call this miniature maneuver "daring" . . . Hey, wait . . . I'm not all that middle class . . . you just can't see the tongue in my cheek when I call this daring . . . though it is daring from the vantage point of propriety in the middle-class set), and then the smiling face said he had thought of doing likewise and offered to follow my lead if I was successful. Whereupon I parked without any problems.

Later, at the dinner, this same man was there and as we had already established a common meeting ground . . . he, following my lead, had also parked his own car . . . it was easy to make a significant contact with him. Now, this may not seem like much, and in fact it's a very little dare in my behavior, but this man turned out to be one of the most interesting men I've met in Miami . . . an inventor, a poet, and an oceanographer, a person whom I found attractive and an enjoyable dinner companion. Without the minor risk I would not have made prior contact with him and would probably not have met him in the large crowded dinner hall. I'm really thrilled at having met this guy. And it's not that he writes Haiku, or that he's smart and good looking, it's that, listening to the music I see in his face, I feel his character shine out . . . he has soul . . . and for a white American to have soul, baby, that's something! And it all started from *getting out of line*.

Have you kept in line all day today? Did you do *anything* out of line? Risk . . . it's a risk to say *no* when you feel *no* . . . it's easier to *act yes* and say *yes* when you *feel no* . . . you women, lying in bed (double entendre intended) . . . putting on your show . . . you know what I'm talking about. To say and act *no* when you feel *no* is definitely a no-no. Be nice. How murderous the stifled *no* becomes under the niceness, the icy niceness . . . do you know how it kills . . . yes, the stifled *no* is a killer . . . it kills marriages

. . . it kills kids and turns them into Portnoys, and it turns their mothers into Mrs. Portnoys.

"Don't say that, it isn't nice!" Have any of you escaped a childhood without this admonition? Have any of you parents escaped telling your kids this, or, just as bad, indicated it somehow? Have any of you failed to get this deadly message across? Goddamn it! Even today, after all the garbage and purification by bleeding that I've been through, I still have to keep a check on my checker, keep vetoing my censor that sits on my shoulder or somewhere . . . maybe in my head . . . and tells me I should stifle a yawn when my patient bores me, force my eyes open when a patient is putting me to sleep. When I plunge and take the risk and tell the patient I'm going to sleep or I'm bored, suddenly he blushes . . . admission of guilt? If I'm nice, we enter a conspiracy . . . I won't tell him he's boring me and he won't tell me I look bored and that he's just beating around the bush. If we keep this game going long enough, why, we don't have to risk *anything*. Of course, nothing constructive is gained by this, no real progress, but my!—how comfortable! When I've risked and told him and after he blushes (movement!) he becomes awake and awakens me and the atmosphere becomes electrical in its movement and wakefulness. And the ridiculous paradox of the whole thing is that my worst fears are *never* realized when I take these personal risks. Rather they usually get me *over* an impasse. So what the hell are we doing being so nice and so phony with one another . . . I tell you we are murderers when we kill the truth of our responsiveness. Most of all, we kill our movement, our wakefulness, our aliveness, our animal selves.

Okay . . . it goes like this, the rationalizations:

First: I'm not supposed to or "should not" be bored or sleepy in your presence . . . it would mean that I'm not interested in you. I should always be wide awake with you no matter what you do. (Is this why we always cover our mouths in public when we yawn?)

Second: If I tell you I'm bored, I will hurt your feelings. Also I might expose that I'm really angry at you for not interesting me

165

and for making me listen to such boring stuff that's putting me to sleep.

Third: If I hurt your feelings you won't like me. If you don't like me . . . why, that's dreadful . . . it means I'm not likable . . . it might even mean I won't like myself. *I measure how I feel about myself by whether or not you like me.* (Wow! get that?) In fact, my survival depends on your liking me. So . . . how can I take such a risk and tell you what you're doing to me? I don't want to *die,* you know. I want to survive at any cost . . . so I have to play it safe . . . as long as I know you like me I can make it, even though I get ulcers, or headaches, or backaches, or get impotent, or can't have an orgasm, or can't feel very much pleasure in anything . . . it's just important to be *nice.* Yes, *nice,* and to have you like me and approve of me.

All right, this is what I do to *myself* when I fall into the *nice* bag, or put an ice bag on my feelings and numb them. What do I do to you? Well, first I let you drone (drown, too) . . . I look at you as if I'm interested and this encourages you to keep droning. And when you're droning, you're weaving a hypnotic web around your own feelings that are packaged away somewhere in storage while you go on with your head trip. With your head on its trip, your feelings in cold storage, and my feelings in nice ice, we, you and I can never meet to melt with each other and we retain a refrigerated distance from each other forever. Amen.

Be nice . . . obey your parents . . . never say no . . . be a good girl—these were the lessons Rose was taught in her childhood and she learned her lessons well. So well that, at the age of fifty-five, after thirty years of restrictive and repressive marriage, she was still smiling, polite, nice, never overtly angry. Instead, she carried a stone weight in her chest and belly while her husband continued to undermine and tyrannize her.

Rose had a weak, helpless, ineffectual mother. Her father was a strict authoritarian who "only had to look at the salt on the table and we would give it to him . . . he never had to talk . . . his look was our command." Rose was so "nice" that at the age of

166

twelve she allowed her father to finger her clitoris, lick and suck her vagina while she held her breath in dread lest her sister, aged ten, would awaken in the next bed. She would lie in bed, fearful of going to the bathroom, lie there "with my bladder near bursting, afraid to go to the bathroom because every time I did my father would be waiting in the dark hall and get me and wouldn't let me go until he played with my vagina." She thus remained frozen in acceptance of his sexual advances for over one and a half years, stifling her shouts and repugnances, living thereafter in her guilt over the orgasms she had thus received . . . "he would never stop playing with me until I had an orgasm."

And later, so confused were the sexual messages she gave her children, beneath her perennial smile, that her son and daughter, in their late teens, continued to have an ongoing incestuous relationship under her very nose . . . (that's nice, don't fight).

The denial of the shout-yell "Don't!"—"I won't!"—is the murderer. This woman carried, for forty-five years, the heavy monument to her stifled shout in her breast and belly and paved the way for her post-adolescent children to screw each other. Before this gravestone could be eliminated, she needed to get rid of her "niceness" and release the unreleased shout. And did she ever yell! It was truly startling to hear the fierce, piercing, wild shouts erupt from this heretofore nice-smiling Rose, to the gradual dissolution of her millstone and automatic smile.

Risk—if I stay in bed I don't have to worry about getting run over by an automobile. Of course, I'll never see the tree on the other side of that dangerous street, and the bluebird will no longer greet me . . . of course, my muscles will atrophy—but slowly— and don't forget, I won't be getting killed all at once and I might not even notice it. How many people go through life with this philosophy? *Play it safe*. All right—I'll be back to this—I can't let it go . . . for life *is* risk, life = risk; no risky, no lifey.

But atrophy . . . (wasting away, you know, when your muscles get wasted from no movement or no innervation . . . ever measure your leg muscles after wearing a cast for several months?) . . .

167

atrophy reminds me of movement. Our whole culture is based on making machines move more and man move less. The more the machines move, the less man has to move. (Has anyone done a study correlating constipation with this phenomenon? The more machines do our movements for us, the less we move, the less, too, our guts move.) People used to look at me askance in New York and Los Angeles when I'd ride through the metropolitan area on a bicycle. Here in Miami Beach, what with tourists vacationing, the locals probably mistake me for a tourist and I get by. So when I rode my daughter to her nursery school in a basket in front of my bike I was not a crazy psychiatrist acting odd. (In a town in Switzerland, the entire village was out on bikes; you could barely get a car through the streets during the time when all the workers were going to work on their bikes.) My motto (another one, that is) is: never ride when I can walk, never lie when I can sit, never sit when I can stand, never float when I can swim. Movement—movement, the expenditure of energy, begets more energy. Did you ever try a fast walk around the block, instead of an aspirin, for a headache? And if once around doesn't do the trick, try two or even three. People are afraid to *move*.

This reminds me of a woman I saw at that posh place on Collins —that benefit dinner—the woman got out of a car as I drove up and she walked into the lobby—she walked as if something would break or get irrevocably out of place if she moved or swung too freely . . . as if some delicate rare object were balanced precariously on her perfectly coiffured high hairdo. Poor dead woman— listen to the loud swish of the blood pumped out of your heart every second . . . tune into the rapid movement of all the things going on inside of you . . . listen to your own rhythm . . . bend, move, swing, glide, slide, rend to the movement inside . . . get your outside in touch with your in . . . come on, risk breaking and I promise you you won't break . . . oh, maybe a strand of that rigid coiffure might get displaced, but dammit, you'll find *your* place in this vast moving universe we're part of. Come on, it's all moving —how about getting into its swing?

Move—what a round, strong word is this—it's the biggest four-letter word I know—it includes that other four-letter word—fuck—and is bigger, more magnitudinous. It is solid and round as the earth, mobile and expansive as the universe. M–O–V–E. When I move the outside of me, I am more in harmony with the phenomenal ever-present movement of my insides. When I am still, I outrage the movement of the least of the billions of cells that make up my whole.

Do you have a headache?—remember to run around the block. Are you constipated?—or have stomach cramps?—go for a bike ride. Are your muscles aching?—go for a swim. Are you depressed?—jump up and down, kick a pillow, pound the bed. Move—move—move—use your energy up and lo!—more is created in double force. Use yourself, bruise yourself, bend and bounce and break yourself—you bounce back longer, mend stronger—move-move-move-move-move-move-move.

You are a motile, mobile animal with voluntary and involuntary muscles—move, man, move.

You are a peristaltic-gutted, heart-pounding, blood-streaming, lung-expanding animal—move, man, move.

Move move move move move move move.

Hey, wait a minute now . . . something that might be misinterpreted by you has just occurred to me. I was just playing around with some ideas in my head: "I think, therefore I am" . . . I move, therefore I am . . . I move, therefore I live . . . I am still, therefore I die . . . when I suddenly thought of a different kind of movement that is like a killing of life . . . a frenetic movement that is discordant with life's rhythms . . . the frenzied, automated movement so well portrayed in the film version of *A Thousand Clowns* . . . the "fever and the fret" of dissonant, nonrelevant movement, whether of the feet or of the mouth . . . the incessant jumping around that really has no contact with the inner consonant movement of a gut in tune with the natural movement of the cosmos. When I urge my patients to move, go, go—get started—to physically and behaviorally get up and get the body moving—

169

move into life—this frenzied moving is there at the other end of the spectrum and acts as a barrier to getting in touch with the inner flow. In gut terms: a gut expression of this chicken-without-a-head-erratic-factory-line-speedup-automated movement would be ulcerative colitis, bloody nonfunctional movement . . . destructive motion.

Agitated motionlessness . . . did you ever see a person suffering from agitated depression? . . . were you, yourself, ever depressed and agitated? . . . with all the purposeless dysfunctional movement . . . this is the time of the real danger of suicide . . . all that purposeless movement finally mustered into one grand purposeful destruction—suicide. In a sense we symbolically commit suicide (and, in degrees, physiologically as well) when we engage in any of those agitated movements. Take eating inordinately and incessantly for example—filling the mouth instead of the loins, turning the energy inward instead of directing its flow outward. What if a fat person, in reaching for a bonbon, were to say: "I really want to suck Mom's tit now, and this bonbon I'm eating is a substitute tit." Or, if there are some elements of displaced genitality involved in the act of eating the bonbon, what if he were to say: "I want to fuck someone and instead I'm masturbating with my mouth, fucking myself in the mouth."

Hell hath no fury like nature betrayed. (The human animal is betraying his nature; hence, the world's present eruption.) When I see a fat person—you know, the jolly fun-loving fat person—I see the vengefulness, vindictiveness, and hostility, packed in those layers of fat, that he turns against himself, outraging his heart, liver, and psyche—all those extra miles of blood vessels his poor, breaking heart has to pump through. Watch out for the fat jolly ones! The lean and hungry Cassiuses and scrawny Iagos with their evident dyspeptic natures don't hold a candle to the murderous rage hidden beneath those fatty layers and smiling jowls of the fat ones.

Or take smoking—another mouth filler and lung filler: "Keep one part moving so all else can die" . . . destructive movement, hand and mouth in their death synchrony. Imagine people equating

170

cigarettes with *life!* "What'd be the use of living if I had to give up smoking?" Life being equated with a cigarette, a drug! Hey!—you got the wrong side of the coin—death is the drug, life the absence of it; death the adulterant, life the pure, the unadulterated—adult —to be the average American adult is to be impure, drugged, deceased . . . then let me keep the primitive child in me alive, unadulterated with adult destructiveness—let me keep my fears, anxieties, timidities, joys, ecstasies, pains—and stay alive, alive-o. Let me suffer and remain intact . . . head, body, psyche, and soul together in a life synchrony, moving beneath my stillness, speaking beneath my silence, feeling beneath my subtle touch. I will not drug myself out of contact with my deadness and my aliveness, with my incapacities and capacities. I will encompass all within me uncompromised by nicotine, caffeine, hash, or pot, alcohol or barbiturates, ups or downs, smack or speed. Here I am in my lonely-companied, glad-sad, scared-brave, celibate-wanton, true-false, mirage-real totality with all its contradictions, and I promise to take me as I am for better or worse, as I am—for as I am is all I am and all there is of me. And I will cherish my tears— without them I know no joy . . . and I will cherish my fears— without them I have no courage. And I will not put them to sleep beneath blankets of tranquillity pills—I will not outrage my nature —I will not put my aliveness to death!

Okay—I give you this: if you go to a doctor and something doesn't sit right with you about how he treats you or about what he is suggesting, goddamn it, don't be "nice" . . . take the risk of hurting his feelings and seek one or a dozen consultations. Are you more interested in *your flesh* or his feelings? One exception here—if you're a hypochondriac, get yourself a good Gestalt or experiential or reality oriented or existential or just plain human therapist and don't shop around for surgeons or you might, like one of my hypochondriacal patients, run into a rash of cutters, surgeons who have their knives ready in their hands before you enter their door and tell your story . . . surgeons whose sole interest lies in keeping their operating schedules full—without holes. Don't be their hole filler! Remember: it's *your flesh* versus their feelings . . . and their feelings, after all, are only related to the business aspect of your body and how it fills the holes in their schedule while their coffers heap up. Be a person, not a hole filler!

Hey, have I maligned too many doctors . . . have I made too many prospective patients anxious? Good!—*be anxious*—be nervous and worried and anxious about your choice of a doctor. Come on now, look around you. Good people are hard to find . . . doctors are people too . . . so never forget how bad or how good they can be. Get that authority mote out of your eye. Your parents are people, your teachers are people, your priests are people, your doctors are people—and you're people. Good, bad, selfish, generous, materialistic, egoistic, humble . . . don't think anyone else is so different from you. Despite his status, remember he gets snot in his nose just like you. If a winter coat isn't warm enough, I won't buy it and freeze . . . I look around until I find a warmer one to buy . . . should I be more meticulous about the external temperature of my body and not the inner climate? I'll shop around for a good doctor . . . I won't sit in his office with my body and be treated like cattle even though he is a famous New York pediatrician with a fabulous reputation (as once I did) . . . I'll find a decent human being for my kids and one who treats me with dignity and not as a coin for his overloaded machine.

I started talking of risks—if it's not worth taking a risk, it's not worth having or doing or being.

I had an experience in that university class I mentioned. I was supposed to teach some Gestalt therapy ideas and views of group interaction; actually, the class turned into a big encounter group flowing and glowing by the end of the term. But somewhere in the middle of the term I ran into a snag . . . I got off on a head trip . . . (A head trip is an intellectualizing, up-in-the-head set of ideas divorced from feelings, from gut responses . . . you middle-class educated intellectuals: do you know how dried up your juices get when you get up in your heads? I'll give you an example: a patient was responding to something I said and she made the following statement: "That has the earmarks of a fault-finding remark"—this is head-trip language. What she meant, when we unmasked her gut reaction, was: "You hurt me when you say that." Incredible, no? The intricacies of such translations, the contortions! You teachers up there, divorced not only from the hundreds of students you are lecturing at but also from yourselves . . . how many of you admit to your students what's happening in your own guts . . . your feelings of being threatened, fearful, angry?)

To get back to my own head trip . . . this was the first class I had taught at university level and I was thrown off keel by thoughts of exams, grades, and attendance, all of which were totally irrelevant to what was the real purpose for my teaching the class, namely to give us all an encounter experience with as much risk taking and intensity as we could tolerate, from which to grow. After the first few groovy class sessions, I began to get didactic and dried up. I no longer felt the enthusiasms and excitements I had felt in the earlier class sessions. There was a gradual process of my becoming more and more "the teacher"—more and more concerned with the prescribed texts—less and less with experiencing the students . . . or myself.

Then suddenly—explosion! The whole class pounced on me, told me I expected all of them to take risks and I was taking none myself, that I held myself back, that I was up in my head, that I made them angry and frustrated. Wow!—what a shaking up! They really got my guts stirred. After a momentary defensiveness with my jaw set and my shoulders hunched, I came clean—told them how threatened I felt, how uptight I had felt about the whole idea of "covering the texts adequately, taking attendance, and so on," and how it had derailed my previous enthusiasms and free-swinging contact. Goddamn!—how the class flowed after that. I reached into myself and exposed them to learning experiences from which they arose excited and inspired . . . motivated. It turned out to be a great experience for me, and I was grateful to the most vociferously angry among them for getting me out of my head . . . those who were most angry later became the most loving.

So remember, you instructors in your dead heads . . . death is when you stay in your heads . . . put the chairs in your class-rooms in a circle and join the circle—a circle has no head and no backs of heads—get face to face . . . remember Rilke's "Song of the Blind Man" where he says: ". . . ihr habt ein Gefuhl von Gesicht zu Gesicht, und das verleitet zur Schonung," which roughly reads: you have a feeling of face to face, and that gives you for-bearance . . . remember, though you are the teacher, you are yet an individual, and above all you are a human being relating to other human beings in, hopefully, face to face contact, eyeball to eyeball . . . you'll be able to see better that students are persons too. And, students, take the risk at the kind of confrontation my students had with me . . . you might find that "teach" is just an-other person with guts like yourselves!

I had a patient who taught English at a college. He was a typical up-in-the-head intellectual—pale face (his blood was all in his brain), stiff body, studied, meticulously correct speech—totally unimpassioned, emotions encased.

Interestingly enough, his hobby was woodworking. We discov-ered that his father (Italian) used to call him "testa dura" (hard head). I wonder whether his chipping away at wood was some self-curative attempt to chip away at and get rid of the hardness of his own head. I wonder, too, whether he screwed his wife with his cranial head and not the more fitting one?

He complained of boredom and unrest in relation to his school-work. His classes had become routinized and deadened and he approached them with considerable anxiety.

In our work of a few months' duration, there was considerable focus on his hard head. In one session I asked him to hit his head against the wall (with a pillow intervening). The petrified nature of his hard head became strikingly clear in this procedure, and the session proved to be the turning point in his therapy. Gradually his head and body softened, allowing a flow not only of his feelings

174

but of his creativity. He returned to his classes with a surge of innovative ideas, immediately got rid of the "teacher at the head of the class" and placed the students in a circle from then on—no heads, all eyeballing one another. He inaugurated a journal idea with all members of the class contributing to the writing, editing, and publishing of the journal. The students were turned on and he became the most popular English teacher in the school.

Hello. I want to touch you with the things I feel about life—living—breathing—joy—pain. Each time I start on a new tack, it winds up in the same place: get up—look up—move—breathe—push—touch—see—question—see more.

Well, here I am, still touting the values of risk taking. I went to San Juan one weekend hoping to see and hear Pablo Casals—the greatest cellist in the world, still going strong at over ninety—conducting a Beethoven program. I arrived on Friday . . . and living at the ocean front in Miami Beach the way I do you'd think I get enough ocean . . . but you're not an ocean nut like me . . . I just can't get enough of it . . . whenever I go somewhere near an ocean, I just gotta go into it if the temperature allows . . . or else see it . . . be near it . . . hear it. It's always different even when I look at it from the same spot, and what a difference from a different locale! I really can't tell you how much I dig the ocean; it's like my own bloodstream. So, I got a little hotel on the ocean, crowded between some big posh joints that I avoid like the plague (why did I say that?—I never caught the plague at the Fontainebleau), and right away went for a swim. I met a young Puerto Rican fellow on the beach who was admiring my swimming (or at least this is what he said . . . which is as good a way as any to start a conversation), and we talked about Pablo and the concert Sunday night—sold out as I expected—with only a slight possibility of standing room. That got me down . . . I had tried to get tickets in advance in Miami but no go . . . but all was not lost. He told me Pablo had a house down the beach and sometimes Pablo hung out in front of it or played his cello in his house . . . for eavesdroppers? . . . and he also gave me the personal stuff that this ninety-three-year-old guy was married to a thirty-five-year-old woman, had been married to her for the past twelve years (that's better than Chaplin!), and that she, Martita, was an accomplished cellist. On the spot I decided to visit him the next day. If I couldn't hear his concert at least I wanted to see him . . . just to see what a guy with that much genius feels like in the seeing, and maybe even hear a couple of cello strains.

The next afternoon . . . rainy . . . I got a lift to his house. As soon as I got out of the car I began to get cold feet—what the hell was I doing there, anyway . . . could I do such a dumb thing as knock on his door and say: Mr. Casals—I just want to look at you? (Someone, I forget who, at a writer's conference told the story of doing this to George Bernard Shaw who, at his doorway, turned his face to the right and said: "Right profil [that's how he pronounced it], left profil, full face," and then closed the door on him . . . after the guy had traveled all the way from America hoping to "see" Shaw!) I kind of hung around in front of Casals's house in the drizzle . . . a simple, pretty house with a nice garden and some dense tropical foliage beyond . . . and I felt like reneging on the whole deal. To give myself time to figure things out . . . and also something to do . . . I pretended to myself to be interested in looking at the tropical plants and trees and smelling the moist junglelike atmosphere of the vegetation . . . and then my eye lit on the front door, which was ajar. The inviting position of the door was a paradox . . . it worked just opposite . . . how can you knock on an open door? . . . and I felt like an intruder if I approached any closer . . . and I did just that . . . walked right up to the door . . . and then just stood there . . . waiting . . . waiting . . . for whom, Godot? . . . stupidly debating should I or shouldn't I? . . . I never did answer the question because Godot, in the person of a smiling housekeeper (wearing an apron—there I go, stereotyping again just like everyone else—couldn't she be the lady of the house and still wear an apron?), appeared at the doorway—I was stuck, "wriggling on a pin"—the point of no return. In agrammatical Spanish, collected on the streets

176

of Los Angeles, Havana, Mexico, I said: "Por favor, quiero ver Señor Casals," which was supposed to mean: "Please, I'd like to see Mr. Casals." In proper Spanish she told me he was sleeping after a rehearsal earlier that day and that Señora Casals might be awake and she'd go see, and before I could object and cut into her speedy flow (are those Spanish people always racing to see how many words they can fit into a single breath—like we used to have races to see who could keep his head in a bucket of water longest? . . . now with my Yoga breathing, it should be easier to win this race at least, but I'd never try to compete in speed of babble with one speaking The Loving Tongue), before I could even breathe, she had disappeared down the dark hallway.

Now I really felt stupid . . . and if the housekeeper went so far as to wake her up!—geez, it'd be hard to live that one down—even though Martita was only thirty-five and not ninety-three, she still needed all the stamina she could get under those circumstances. I decided I was beyond redemption—ridiculous—but how can you be alive and not feel ridiculous sometimes? Martita appeared quickly and didn't look sleepy . . . so I again took up the cudgel of my self-taught Spanish and introduced myself, apologized for disturbing her, said something about how I had hoped to see her husband at the Sunday concert and it was sold out and had she any suggestions. She was a pretty woman, sweet-natured, said something about standing-room possibilities (I think—that tripping-tongued racing again! —she assumed I knew more Spanish than I do because my accent is good . . . the street's the best teacher you can find . . . so she kept in high gear), and then invited me to a full rehearsal that very night! I would have bowed down before her on the spot if I felt she would have appreciated such a gesture—abundantly thanked her—and flew off.

That night was a real treat . . . even more so than a dress performance . . . at the University of Puerto Rico theatre. The musicians were almost all in shirt-sleeves—disheveled and sloppy looking as they would be on a summer night hanging around their kitchens. They were milling on the stage, tuning up, kidding with one another

177

—a casual, informal family gathering—a motley crew. The audience scattered around the auditorium, also informal, about thirty or forty among the thousands of seats.

And then suddenly I felt an awe . . . there was a short, bent, decrepit old man escorted very-very-very slowly to a three-legged stool at center stage (by Alexander Schneider, as it turned out). Once on the stool, Casals remained there till the end of Beethoven's *Egmont* Overture, conducting the motleys who, under his direction, turned suddenly into a homogeneous voice praising Beethoven, Egmont, Casals, and whatever gods may be. And there, among the violins, was Schneider—piss and vinegar, energetic, vibrant in a sweaty shirt—making the music quiver and me too. I sat in the second row, quivering, glowing, bubbling.

Intermission—and I went back stage to get closer to Casals and just in time to see Martita help his wretched body into a chair, hover over him like a mother bird, and peck a kiss at his temple— while he settled his stiff joints into some least painful position. I caught the spirit of this man—that had flowed out into each musician and out through their instruments—that was still there, flowing out of his small, glowing eyes . . . a giant in a bowed, pygmy form. I hung around—gawking I admit—never taking my eyes off him—not daring to move closer and bombard him with any further demand—I felt an adoration for him—wanted to touch him with a word or handshake—and stayed in my own orbit while I watched the others gather round him. I'm sorry now I didn't touch him in some way—he sure touched me!

Intermission over—and out comes a guy with shirt flopping over his pants—Isaac Stern—looking like someone's pudgy uncle . . . you couldn't even notice his nonexistent chin the way he bowled you over with his violin playing . . . if you play a violin like *that,* man, who even notices if you've got a chin at all?—nobody's looking— yeah, the ears are doing all the looking that's necessary . . . besides, a strong hard chin might be a handicap to a violinist—it wouldn't snuggle so softly into the chin rest.

Then came Leonard Rose with his cello—unique in his suit and proper tie—what the well-dressed musician will wear—guess the decorum of the stately cello rubbed off on him . . . it *is* hard to picture a sloppy Joe playing a cello.

And there . . . obese and sloppiest of all . . . came a stage-hand approaching the piano—I thought he was going to move it (stereotyping again, Eileen!)—but instead of shoving it around, he sat and flowed his fingers over it like soap bubbles—Eugene Istomin. These three bent beneath Casals's direction, yielding . . . then becoming whispering, laughing schoolboys whenever Pablo stopped to correct the orchestra, yielding again to Casals and the Triple Concerto for Piano, Violin, and Cello.

The next morning I was back again for another rehearsal . . . this time at my own invitation. Casals wasn't there, but—or maybe because of this—I got closer to Schneider and Istomin after rehearsal—shaking hands with them, touching their flesh with my own, their eyes with mine . . . and I got to see them clearer: the big, hulking Istomin . . . sensitive . . . tentative . . . shy . . . embarrassed at such close range without a piano to protect him . . . gentle; Schneider . . . bold, bursting, piercing, Mephistophelian . . . twinkle-eyed. Fabulous!

Hey—see what happens when you step out of line . . . upset protocol . . . take a risk . . . dare reach out in a human way to another human being . . . even in an awkward way . . . despite his greatness . . . because of it?

And more than risk taking here is contact . . . which brought me the touch of Istomin's round, withdrawing hand . . . I may forget the music they played, but never the look of Schneider's eye, the touch of Istomin's hand . . . human instruments of the muse . . . just by literally reaching out my own hand. And in some damn way this reaching out, touching these musicians, brings me closer to my own muse—whoever she is. When I risked reaching out, these musicians became simply human . . . in the process I became more alive, more human. The process of humanizing is intimately tied to risk taking, to reaching out.

Pablo, I reach out and salute you. May my energy flow to its

179

creative potential after my body's decline—as does yours. I am
your devoted admirer.

Advice to Lovers

Ah, Lad—
whose arms, though charred,
yet, yet reach yearning . . .
whose heart, though scarred
by her, keeps burning:
Reach, reach, nor cease
despite her spurning;
Love's wisdom you
by this are learning.

Once I, like you,
a maiden cherished;
But pride was King:
Thence all love perished.
And now my arms,
intact and free,
alone embrace
my idiocy.

9

THERAPY:
THE POUND OF CURE

As for therapy: we are on a life
raft, you (as patient) and I (as
therapist) . . . all that you are—do
and feel—affects me . . . all that I
am affects you.

Our raft's making it is as essentially related to you as it is to me.

When you and I ultimately realize
that we are on the same life raft,
therapy is finished.

I want to get to a here and now thing. It was a blast (well, not
all that great, really—it's one of those words that I get from some
of my hip patients that seep in and remain as part of my unthinking
vocabulary) to discover the HAN Institute stands for Here and
Now. I had a fantasy a while back of writing a book showing the

here and now experiential-existential approach in therapy by using an imaginary patient with the following introductory dialogue:

Patient: Help me, Doc—I'm drowning.

Doctor: You're drowning?

Patient: Yes, Doc—I need your help.

Doctor: Here and now?

Patient: Yes, here and now I need your help.

Doctor: Here and now you're drowning?

Patient: Well, no . . . I'm not actually drowning . . . I'm sitting in your office, but I feel like I'm drowning.

Doctor: Here and now?

Patient: Well, maybe not here and now exactly.

Doctor: What exactly *are* you experiencing here and now?

Patient: Well, I'm aware of sitting in this chair and my hands are resting on the arms of the chair and my legs are stretched out in front of me.

Doctor: And what feelings are you in touch with?

Patient: Well, actually (laughs) I feel pretty relaxed.

Doctor: Not drowning?

Patient: (Laughing more) Well no—I feel pretty good in fact.

Doctor: You look pretty good to me. I feel relaxed myself just looking at you.

I would like to share a real "here and now" encounter with a patient that happened not face to face but on the telephone. Some of my most creative interactions with patients take place on the phone. When a patient calls up in a panic or acute distress, I know I have to muster all my sensibilities to get through, and I have to do it immediately. I have to listen to the underground message . . . opening my ears as big as tunnels . . . and when the patient has finally gotten through to me I have to figure out (or rather feel out) what I have to use with this particular person to get through in return. Nancy called me and the following conversation took place:

N: Listen, Eileen . . . (I encourage all patients, no matter what their age, to call me by my first name, and I do likewise) . . . I'm really in bad shape . . . this time I'm really going crazy.

E: How?

N: I'm sitting here staring at three walls and they're closing in on me.

E: What are you doing about it?

N: Nothing, just sitting here looking at the walls.

E: Do you want to go crazy?

N: Sometimes I think it would be nice.

E: Here and now? Do you want to go crazy here and now? Do you want to go to a loony bin?

N: It would be easy.

E: Who's talking about being *easy?* (N laughs) Of course, it would be easy . . . being in a loony bin is easier than being in the outside world. (N laughs more) . . . I'm not talking about *easy*. I want to know if you want to go to a loony bin. You can if you want to, but you don't have to . . . the choice is up to you.

N: (Audibly relieved) No, I don't want to go crazy.

E: What do you *have* to do now?

N: Well, I have to clean my house . . . my friend is coming over soon and I promised to do some sewing with her and show her some stitching techniques.

E: And what do you *plan* to do?

N: (Laughing loudly) I'm going to get to work.

E: It's not easy?

N: No, it's work . . . it doesn't have to be easy. I feel good now. Thanks a lot.

E: You sound good now.

N: I love you. Good-bye.

E: Here's a hug for you, Nancy.

N: I got it. Thanks.

E: Good-bye, see you tomorrow.

David came to see me referred by another psychiatrist. He was a twenty-eight-year-old intelligent, good-looking, but inert man working as a salesman. He was mixed up about his sexual feelings, preferring women but seeming always to get involved with quick, guilt-ridden, unfulfilling sexual encounters with one homosexual after another. He had no overt effeminate characteristics. He led an isolated life, desirous and fearful of going out; he had very few friends, and those he had were as dull and listless and inactive as he—a typical "what are ya doin' tanight, Marty?" crowd. The weekends were the worst time for him and he greeted them with dread. His work week was also dreadful—he really did not like selling—so there was no bright respite from his pleasureless, tension-ridden, unfulfilled life. He had been in psychiatric and psychoanalytic treatment for some years, he had spent some time at Menninger's, and his chronic depression and lack of joy and drive had never lifted.

At his first visit with me, he looked like a dead man—his voice was lifeless, his body flaccid, his face expressionless, his eyes dull. The most obvious thing about him was his utter immobility. He said he had run the gamut of traditional psychotherapeutic approaches and had heard I do something "different." We did something different all right. By the end of that visit, I had him moving, pounding the couch, kicking, breathing, jumping rope with me, moving, moving, moving. He felt something had happened in that session that he had never experienced before and he left in an exhilarated mood. After a few more sessions of much movement and some talk of his being such a nice-obedient-good-boy-who-aimed-to-please, I asked him to externalize his bad-rebellious-devil-may-care boy hiding beneath and carry on a dialogue between him and the good boy. The rebel, at first meek and not very rebellious, got somewhat strengthened during this dialogue . . . and so did the good boy. We moved back to zero position. After a few more uneventful sessions, I began to feel it was mandatory to deal with his wall of blahness, but I didn't immediately see a way through. Then, in his next session, as I continued feeling my way, I found myself getting dull, apathetic, and sleepy. He droned on in his usual monotone until I just couldn't stand the feeling of deadness in myself anymore, so I jumped up and began pacing around as we continued our discussion. Pacing didn't help much until I increased the rapidity of my stride and then I felt my body waking up, becoming lively again. I then told him what I had been feeling, why I suddenly started pacing, and what I was feeling now. I asked him to get in touch with his deadness, how dead his voice sounded, how passive and lifeless his body was feeling. Together, we explored the way he has of protecting himself against contact with people by walling himself in and walling them out, mesmerizing them into boredom and apathy as had happened to me, and thus at once disarming his potential attacker and protecting himself by his withdrawal.

After he more fully contacted his deathlike defensive wall, I invited him to stand up and move. Then, facing him, and standing about one and a half feet away, I talked to him, looking him in the eye. He began to perspire, his death pallor reddened and his face became more alive, his voice more alert, his demeanor more tense and anxious. The flaccidity was gone. The animal on guard was awakened and out there. I moved a step closer . . . his tension increased, the perspiration poured out. As we talked about his increasing tension, I moved closer . . . and closer . . . until I was about an inch away, still looking in his eyes. His awkwardness and embarrassment and anxiety increased . . . so did his aliveness. We talked about contact, fear of it, and his wish to push me back. After a while I invited him to push me back to a comfortable distance, which he did very gingerly. We spent the rest of the session back and forth in this manner, talking of his fears of contact, his fears of pushing away, and his succumbing to immobility, caught between the two extremes.

The weekend following this session, he pushed back . . . and refused to spend another deadly weekend with a couple at whose dull and dulling company he had previously clutched every weekend for fear of being alone, and the following weekend he got really daring and went to a meeting of a quasi-social nature at a small church. Now, after about two months of treatment, he is on the way to standing on his own two feet, actively pushing his drones off, reaching toward more feelingful and alive relationships.

Now, I don't believe it was any of the specific things *I did* with

David that got him moving toward his strength but rather my *involvement* with him that moved him forward. I'm convinced that *no psychiatric tool (technique) ever cured a patient!*—just as no shovel ever dug a hole. It takes a *person* to use that tool. In psychiatry, if the person substitutes the tool for himself, there is no cure—there is only disaster. Look at the poor results in psychiatric and psychoanalytic treatment and you'll see what I mean. Analysis is no tool for *therapy* at all—as I've said, it's great for dissecting dead tissues. Gestalt techniques are great tools for live people, but I've seen them used by mechanical robot men and women in a "psychologically proper" and humanly destructive manner. Bioenergetic therapy provides additional important tools, but I've seen people break down from the therapist's focus on the technique and lack of focus on the person being techniqued. Yes, I've seen bioenergetic analysis applied en masse to the exhilaration of the group at large and to the disintegration of the individual in the group. On the other hand, even an analyst may move his patient toward health if he is human and doesn't allow his tools to robotize him. *There just is no substitute for heart to heart, gut to gut human interaction.* No therapy can really work without it . . . nor can any relationship, for that matter, whether it's man-woman, parent-child, teacher-student, ruler-ruled, or any other.

> So—Don't tool me with your tools
> Don't *treat* me
> Relate to me . . . share with me . . .
> Be real . . . be human with me.

When the so-called patient can say those things to the so-called therapist, when they can both drop the roles they play with each other and relate simply as two persons, the cure is almost achieved. Since it takes two to tango, it is understandable that psychotherapists who won't be persons with their patients defeat their patients' drive toward health, and vice versa. I don't include here the therapists who screw their patients—those I've met give me the impression they do this *not* in the interests of the *person* of their patients, and the ones I've met have never particularly inspired my respect for them as persons.

Before we move on, and while David is finding contact with his aliveness through his emergent anxiety, I'd like to make another plea for anxiety. So—hello, anxiety, I welcome your emergence; you are nature's warning signal and growth potentiator. When I blanket my contact with life's processes (working, achieving, growing, creating, struggling, hating, loving, fighting, being) via all the allures of our drug age, I smother my breathing contact with my life's flow. Only by removing the blanket can I contact my naked anxiety. This anxiety is my inner self-preservative life-wisdom, in the making for those millions of years, sending me a vital message. As the message gets more intensified, I can choose either to ignore it (most efficiently by drugs) or listen to it. If I follow the former course, I need more and more drugs and drug substitutes to keep the message squelched. If I listen, pay attention to the anxiety, the discomfort, the pain, I come face to face with (confront) the underlying block that is destroying my ability to grow and I find at the same time a means of overcoming that block. As long as I drug myself out of this type of awareness, I cannot find it, and I stay wrapped in my safe cocoon of substitute tranquillity, substitute peace, substitute life.

So . . . whereas most people (patients and therapists, doctors, drug companies, etc.) react to anxiety as though it were a "bad" thing, a no-no to rid themselves of by whatever drug or other means is available, I approach its emergence as a sign of life being threatened, a tugging at the person's consciousness to sit up and take notice and *do something,* a warning of a conflagration, an announcement of a life-destructive process that must be immediately uncovered, dealt with, and reversed. (Hans Selye, I salute you.)

Now—it is true that there are situations to which we may respond with crippling anxiety, anxiety so overwhelming that it floods the entire system and breaks down any attempt to function. These anxieties, in particular, are best dealt with via a particular

187

type of graded confrontation that I'll describe. But the underlying principle of confrontation and dealing with our anxieties remains: it is via these confrontings that we sponsor our growth, and via avoiding these confrontings that we encourage our decay.

As for ways of confronting overwhelming anxiety, I owe many thanks to the ideas of J. Wolpe, Jay Haley, Viktor Frankl, M. Erickson, and F. Perls, and to the person of my mother. Later, the fearless encountering approach of Tom Stampfl and John Rosen was to influence me further. One day I was confronted with a patient's desperate situation. Brenda, twenty-one years old, in treatment with me for about nine months, arrived in a severe anxiety state associated with LSD flashback experiences. These flashbacks (nightmarish hallucinations) were frequent and occurred unpredictably, associated with convulsive movements, tremors, terrible and frightening hallucinations, and overwhelming dread. She was an ex-heroin addict who had been hooked on every kind of drug in and out of the book; she had also been an alcoholic. She had been on over a hundred LSD trips. Her father, who was separated from her mother, was an alcoholic; her mother was a very self-righteous, "helpful," lecturing and sermonizing martyr type—the typical wife of an alcoholic—who essentially rejected Brenda.

So there was Brenda, fit to be tied, finding the recurrent flashbacks intolerable . . . and there was I with no knowledge of what to do with flashbacks since all psychiatrists I had heard on the subject admitted that there was no real cure, just medication or high dosages of one of the vitamin B complexes to give a flushing reaction from which some patients seemed to get minimal relief, if any. I felt helpless. But I decided to try some stuff I had put together from my readings and experience. Here's the session, as best I can recall it: (At the time of this session, Brenda had been off all drugs for four months.)

E: Would you like to work on your flashbacks?

B: Yeah—they're real bad—I'd sure like to get rid of them.

E: All right—would you just relax as deeply and completely as you can.

B: (Closing her eyes and resting her head on the back of the chair) Yeah, that's easy for me—I just turn my eyes inside and look at a spot in the middle of my brain—I've done a lot of auto-hypnosis.

E: Now, staying with your attention focused on the core in the middle of your brain, let your mind travel over your body and seek out any areas of tension, any tight places, any rigidities . . . and release them . . . let go of them. Stay in focus on your brain and become aware of your entire body from top to toe, outside and inside, and find any places where you are tight . . . and release the tension. Now—staying in your state of deep relaxation, let me know when you have achieved this. You will be able to talk with me while remaining profoundly relaxed.

B: (Visibly relaxed) OK.

E: You are completely relaxed?

B: I feel a little tight here (points to upper midabdomen).

E: All right—let your abdomen become more tense—try to tighten it more—increase the tension there as much as you possibly can.

B: (Visibly straining) Uh huh.

E: And when you have tightened it as much as you think you can, go a step further and tighten it even more.

B: (Straining more . . . clenching jaw muscles, hands clutching arms of chair . . . pause . . . finally stops straining, relaxes, stretches arms and legs out)

E: And now?

B: (Takes deep breath) I feel better.

E: And your abdomen?

B: It's no longer tight.

E: Good! Now once again become aware of your body's relaxation. What do you feel now?

B: I feel relaxed—my stomach isn't tight any more . . . I feel real good. (Smiles)

E: All right. Now, staying in touch with your good feelings and your relaxation, I'd like you to recall the most mild flashback ex-

189

perience you've ever had . . . when you feel your stomach tightening, get rid of the flashback experience and focus on relaxing your stomach . . . when you've achieved this, visualize the flashback again . . . continue going back and forth until you can imagine the entire flashback experience while remaining relaxed and feeling good. (Long pause)

B: (Smiles . . . eyes still closed) OK.

E: Good . . you were successful in maintaining complete relaxation and good feelings while fantasizing the entire flashback experience?

B: Yes. (Still smiling)

E: All right . . . now on a scale of tension from zero to 100, zero being complete relaxation and 100 being extreme or total tension, where would you say the tension connected with that flashback experience should be placed?

B: Around 40.

E: All right—on the scale, where would you be now?

B: Zero.

E: Now—I'd like you to think of another and more disturbing flashback that you've experienced before—bring back the entire flashback—tell me where you reach on the scale . . . and then repeat the process you've just been through, stopping the flashback when you go above zero tension and returning to the flashback when you come back to zero again. Keep up the process until you can fantasize the entire flashback without rising above zero tension.

B: (Long pause . . . some intermittent evidence of tensing up muscles) OK.

E: What level of tension would you say this flashback started with?

B: About 60.

E: All right—would you like to go on?

B: Yes.

E: At what level do you want to work out?

B: 100.

E: Good! Now visualize the worst flashback experience you've ever had . . . one that you were having convulsions with . . . and repeat the process . . . imagine the absolutely worst and most horrible flashback you've ever had.

B: (Some visible struggle with intermittent twitches of her face . . . long pause . . . then smiles faintly) OK.

E: You are able to confront a 100 level flashback and overcome it?

B: (Beaming proudly . . . eyes still closed) Yes.

E: Terrific! Would you like to go still one step further?

B: Yes.

E: I'd like you to imagine a flashback experience worse than any you've ever really experienced—a horrible bummer—and once you've achieved this fantasy, go through the same process of confronting it and removing it when the tension goes above zero, until you can face it fully while maintaining full and complete relaxation at zero tension. (Long pause . . . signs of struggle, intermittent muscle twitching, obvious disturbance)

B: OK. (smiling broadly)

E: What are you feeling now?

B: I'm feeling good and relaxed.

E: You can handle your flashbacks?

B: Yes.

E: So now you have a tool you can use when you leave here—you can get rid of your flashbacks when they are too disturbing or you can allow them to return and still stay in touch with your good feelings and your relaxation.

B: That's great!

E: You can open your eyes when you're ready and still retain your relaxation if you wish.

B: (Opens eyes slowly—breathing deeply and regularly) Thanks —I feel great.

One week later, Brenda said: "I've been getting to sleep without trouble since our session for the first time in months." She had one minor flashback experience during the first week following that session and was able to ward it off with minimal anxiety. Following this one mild episode, she remained completely free of all flash-back experiences to the time of this writing, which is almost two years following that session which, incidentally, was of approximately forty-five minutes' duration. Prior to that session, she had had the flashbacks for months as frequently as four to five times a week.

Brenda and I had been through the mill together with severe verbal harangues and fights . . . once or twice she had felt on the verge of flattening me out when I angered her. She's a strong ox and could easily have wiped me out. But gradually she learned to trust me and let me in. She had tested me to the hilt and finally, finally accepted me. Without her trust and acceptance I doubt that we would have had the successful results.

The clincher and turning point in our relationship occurred several months earlier when she had been off drugs for a short time. She had had an argument with her Mother-Bitch, which always brought her in furious at me, and she entered my office on the war-path. (I had a prescription pad with about five Rx's left in it on a small table to the side of our chairs. I keep this handy for writing down appointment times, when necessary; books I'm recommending, dosages of natural organic vitamins, names of trustworthy doctors I'm recommending, job contacts I might know about, and various and sundry other communications.)

Just after sitting down, looking fierce, she suddenly lunged forward and grabbed the pad:

E: C'mon, Brenda . . . put it down . . . cut the crap.

B: (Belligerent, psychopathic smile) You gonna make me?

E. No—you're gonna make yourself. Now come on and put it down.

B: I'm just gonna take this with me and have me a good time.

We established very soon how furious she was with her mother, but this didn't help our immediate situation. As we talked, my mind leaped to all possible solutions. One was an awareness that from a *practical* point of view she could really get whatever drugs she wanted, so why get so excited about five lousy prescription blanks?

This was a safe, easy, contemptible cop-out, which I soon dismissed. I knew that, no matter what, I would not let her out of my office without making an attempt to get those back. I knew, at the same time, how dangerous a direct physical conflict would be—she was about sixty pounds heavier and huskier than I and I knew how violent she could be, especially now with her fury at her mother at its height. Her mother had hospitalized her in a psychiatric hospital against her will and somehow she always feared that her mother (and I as her accomplice) might do this to her again. My mind leaped to easier solutions—I was pretty sure I could distract her by our conversation and then make a grab at it (she dangled it loosely on her lap during our session and I sat facing her not more than three feet away), but this, too, I dismissed. I couldn't be sneaky about it . . . there was nothing to do but directly confront her, straight and square. I had fleeting thoughts of going into the next room to call the police and knew simultaneously I would not do this either. A last resort in my meanderings to get away from the direct and possible physical confrontation was the thought of having my next patient help me get the pad from her, but then I had the image of that patient—a young, slim, featherweight, pale, frightened young man who would probably have fainted dead on the spot.

No—there was no substitute and no escape. We got to the end of the session and again, as we were rising from our chairs, I asked her to give me the pad, and I got her expected "No." Then I suddenly grabbed her heavy, stocky arm with my ample peasant hand (there's a value in scrubbing kitchen floors after all) and held on with all my force, while I looked her squarely in the eyes: "Brenda, listen . . . I want that pad . . . and I don't want to fight you . . . I know you can smatter me—both you and I know that—and if I have to get smattered, OK—but I don't want you to leave with that pad." I kept my grip firmly on her arm. She tensed up momentarily, then dropped the pad on the floor—I wasn't going to take any chance on picking it up at that moment. I released my grip on her arm and she moved toward the door. I moved quickly toward her and grabbed her hand. "Thanks, Brenda—I'll see you next week."

I was thoroughly shaken for several minutes so that my pallor and frailty fully equaled that of my next patient. But after that session there was a change in Brenda. She was never distrustful of me again, and the following week she moved her chair close to mine (she had always ostentatiously backed up her chair at a greater distance than most of my other patients), and a few weeks after that she embraced me as she was leaving, having been deathly afraid of any show of fondness toward anyone.

In my work I see over and over again that the sedative head-in-the-sand approach (tranquilizers are the extreme form of this approach and its logical absurd conclusion), avoiding the anxious confronting, is in itself the very essence of the pathological process; whereas the direct confrontation, head-on, with the fearful and the anxious is the process most successful in a healthy life and a healthy therapy.

A forty-nine-year-old man, Gary, came to see me with an airplane phobia that was so severe he even refused to let his grown-up children fly anywhere. When he offered them trips, they had to take other means of travel. We decided to spend one session confronting his excessive fear of flying. Seated in a chair in front of him, I asked him to close his eyes and tune in to his breathing, his body, his feelings. I asked him to picture the pleasant aspects of airplane travel, perhaps the music on an overseas flight, the comfort of the seat, the beautiful vista from the window. Then something like the following dialogue took place, after he was sufficiently relaxed:

E: What's the worst thing that could happen to you in an airplane?

G: I could crash (visibly getting tense with this).

E: All right. I'd like you to visualize taking an airplane and having it crash.

G: Oh, no! (Laughs tensely)

194

E: I believe it will help you.

G: Must I?

E: Of course not. You can go on living with your flying phobia.

G: Well, all right. What should I do?

E: Are you ready to work?

G: Go ahead.

E: Then visualize yourself getting into the airplane and tell me everything you experience until the final crash—use the present tense—tell me it as it's happening.

G: (Eyes still closed, hands resting on arms of chair) Well, I get on the plane, there's a pretty stewardess showing me where to go (smiles). I sit in my seat and fasten my seat belt. I hear the motor revving up and I'm getting nervous. (He grips the arms of the chair, obviously tensing up.) The plane is going up and I'm getting more nervous. (Long pause—he is clutching the arms of the chair tighter, his face in a horrified grimace, his eyes very tightly closed . . . then his entire body begins to shake jerkily reaching a crescendo.) It's over. (His body stops jerking.)

E: And now?

G: I'm dead. (Visibly relaxed)

E: What do you feel now?

G: Nothing—I'm dead. (Pause) I feel relaxed. (Opens eyes) That was some ordeal! (Smiles faintly)

E: You did a good job. Just enjoy the feeling of being relaxed. (Pause) Ready for more work now?

G: Uh, I guess so.

E: All right, let's repeat the whole process.

G: Oh no! I can't!

E: You don't want to work on your airplane phobia?

G: Yes I do, but . . . do I have to do it again?

E: You don't have to, but it would help work through your phobia if you did.

G: It's hard work—almost unbearable.

E: I know.

G: OK (resigned). What should I do?

E: Go through the crash again—you can skip some of the pre-liminaries.

G: (Closing his eyes) I'm sitting on the plane with my seat belt fastened. We're rising off the ground. Now we're flying in the air. The motor suddenly stops and we're falling . . . we're going to crash! (He juts his legs out, feet pushing into the floor as if preparing for a crash, he holds on to the arms of the chair tightly and rigidly, his entire body is tensed, tremulous, somewhat jerky . . . then he relaxes . . . pause . . .) It's over.

E: And now?

G: (Opens his eyes) I feel relaxed (smiles). I'm glad it's over . . . I feel pretty good.

E: So you survived your fear of crashing and you feel pretty good now?

G: Yes.

E: Good. Ready for one more time?

G: I don't want to, but I'll do it.

E: Great! (G repeats the process, but with much less tension during the crash scene.)

At the end of the session, Gary felt strong and as though he had accomplished something. The following weekend he flew with his wife to an island in the Caribbean, and a few months later his daughter flew to Europe with his blessing—all without his anxiety or concern. He had confronted his fears and anxieties about flying in a head-on collision and he wound up *enjoying* an airplane flight for the first time in his life.

Confrontation—the magic and miracle of the head-on gut-on collision . . . beautiful! And—it works!

I approached a northern white man's racism in much the same manner, namely confronting his fearful fantasies. His racism turned out to be a phobic reaction to black men. He had fantasies of the black man's ripping his belly apart with a knife and then ripping his wife apart by raping her with a thick, yard-long penis. After confronting his wild fears in a head-on collision by getting him to take the part, in fantasy, of the black raper splitting his own wife apart, he got in touch with tormented inadequacy feelings as a male and his aggressive and hostile feelings toward his domineering, pushy wife. Within two weeks of this session he stopped using the word "nigger" and began criticizing people in his social milieu who used the word and who held views he himself had held just prior to that session. He began reading books on black history and began defending the black viewpoint at his white upper-middle-class social gatherings.

I experienced a classical example of the dynamics of racism in a session with a fairly religious Jewish woman in her twenties, mother of two girls. She sat in her usual way in our sessions—directly opposite me, face to face. Each time with a patient I notice something I hadn't seemed to notice previously—as if it takes time for a total personality to come into one's consciousness. For the first time in our contact, I noticed that she kept her head tilted to the right side. In response to my question: "What does Right mean to you?" she immediately responded: "Conservative, Ku Klux Klan, John Birch, racial prejudice." I asked whether she felt she was racially prejudiced, and she answered: "Well, yes . . . I wouldn't want my children to interdate or marry a Negro . . . I don't want them to mix their blood."

As we went on in our discussion, it developed that she had a fear that black men might rape her. In my usual way of confronting any fear, I had her live out, in fantasy, the thing feared, namely, the rape by a black man. She developed the picture of a black man, a janitor, in a basement coming after her, grabbing her, ripping her clothes off and throwing her on the ground and ramming a giant black penis up her. At this moment, with her eyes closed and her face contorted in tension, her feeling of fear precipitously changed to one of sensual pleasure, and the tense tight look on her face was replaced by a relaxed smile accompanied by her statement: "I like it." After the fantasy scene was completed, she said: "I feel vibrating all over." She then admitted having felt sexual arousal by looking at the father of one of her daughter's black schoolmates whom she had invited to her daughter's birthday party.

So the layers of racism in this patient were simply and clearly revealed: Layer one: commands to her children such as: "Don't interdate black people—we believe in equality of opportunity but not intermarriage." (*Any line between peoples eventually becomes a noose with which to hang the "outsider."*) Layer two: fear of rape by a black man. Layer three: sexual curiosity, excitement ("vibration"), and desire for a black man.

In the session the following week she said: "I've been thinking it over and I really don't think I can judge whether it's right or wrong for my daughter to marry a black man—that's her decision. My job is to bring her up and teach her good things in life . . . the rest is up to her."

Beneath another patient's rat phobia was the fantasy that they would eat into her vagina and gnaw at the insides of her body. Again, a confrontation with the elements in her fantasy by getting her to play the part of the rat whom she had gnawing into her vagina, getting inside her body, and eating her brain resulted in a marked decrease of her excessive fear and repulsion toward rats. She also discovered some extremely hostile, enraged feelings during the association with the gnawing rats.

Confront your fantasies . . . take responsibility for them . . . they are yours. Once you own your fantasies, you have cured yourself of the fear. And if you must seek help in confronting yourself, don't jump into the arms of the first available psychiatrist.

I had a neighbor-friend in Los Angeles, Alan, whom I tried, at his request, to refer to psychiatrists, and failed three times. From the first consultation with the first psychiatrist, Alan came back and said: "He's in worse shape than I am," and like a light I saw that it was true—the doctor had an aggressive, domineering wife and he himself was passive, indirect, and evasive—a mama's boy. On the second referral, an analyst, the doctor agreed to see Alan once a week, but when he found out Alan had more money than he had originally confessed, the analyst got angry and insisted on seeing him at least three times a week. This turned us both off this doctor whose anger was financially self-serving. The third doctor turned out to be an aggressive, hard, cold, masculinized woman who was altogether too much to stomach for anyone with a heart and a sacred attitude toward his balls. So, after these three failures I decided to give it a try. He was the first friend I had ever treated professionally, and I started with some misgivings . . . it confounded all the protocol I had been taught, protocol that dictated that the psychiatrist should never take his friends in treatment, nor members of his own family, nor even members of his patient's family, and above all that he should keep a social distance from his patients at all times. (Today I see this protocol as so much crap . . . many of my patients become my friends while in treatment and there's great rapport and also speedy progress . . . also I've given sessions to members of my immediate family and only good came out of these. So I have no remaining hangups on this score. In fact, as I've already mentioned, until the doctor can become humanized, there's a gap of unfinished business . . . treatment isn't finished until the patient can see the doctor as a human being with clay feet, and the child doesn't really mature until he can do likewise with his parents.)

Anyway, Alan was a pleasureless guy, a hard-working young lawyer with a wife and two kids . . . a guy who didn't do anything to rock the boat or get out of line anywhere. He worked at a law firm where he played the part of a white Uncle Tom, yassuh'ing his bosses and even his co-workers and secretaries. After treatment commenced, his first breakthrough was a physical one—he began running around the block in Beverly Hills where he lived (it was in the "poor section" of Beverly Hills, south of Wilshire Boulevard, but Beverly Hills nonetheless) . . . running every day in front of whatever neighbors were out . . . and he really got turned on . . . by the movement . . . by the fact of doing his thing before jogging became as fashionable and as acceptable as golf . . . and by doing it, by heck, smack on the pavements of Beverly Hills where cops will stop and question you if you even hold your head a little funny!

199

Don't forget, this was a guy who could never stand to have any fun . . . who felt guilty at the slightest pleasure. He later allowed himself to take up tennis and began to have great pleasure from this. He began to realize for the first time how immobile, how pleasureless his life had been. And most of all—he became more aggressive, he began to say *no* when he felt *no* (even to his boss)— do you hear the movement in this? . . . the ability to push back . . . to say *no* . . . to push back. (One aftermath of his pushing back was that he shortly thereafter got a substantial raise at his job.)

Hey, out there, can you push back? Will you push back? Pushing back . . . "no" . . . "I won't" . . . "I like me" . . . Can you do or say these things?

How many people I see who won't push back, how many crushed personalities who will not, even upon request, say the words: "I like me."

I have developed an interesting interplay I use with some patients: when a new patient seems to be passive, fearful, too nice, too polite, and refuses or seems unable to say "I like me," I play a little game. We stand up facing each other and put our hands out and we take turns pushing each other (that is, pushing back, the physical counterpart of the verbal *no*-saying, of the "I won't . . . I like me . . . I won't be a pushover") . . . and we take turns either resisting the other's pushing or giving in to it. Interestingly enough, the most paranoid patient I ever treated in an out of the hospital setting . . . who was very bitter and verbally attacking and had plans to kill off the Communists, or the Jews (she made an exception in my case), or the Fascists, or the Catholics, or the Protestants . . . with all this verbal barrage, she was unable to push me back at all. She would put up her hands and weakly maintain them in the air and her ferocity vanished. She probably equated pushing me back with killing me. Do you recognize this fear in yourself? If you push me back, do you kill me? Is your *no* so powerful that you annihilate me with it? How weak do you think I am if I die with your mere pushing me back, with your mere *no*. Come—push me back—when you push me back, I feel my own strength—you help make me strong when you push me back—I feel your strength when I push you back—I want us to push each other back—only then can we really merge—but as two strengths—not fallen apart and staying apart as two unpushed, unpushing weaknesses.

Contact—I touch my patients' hands—they touch mine—our strengths combine in the pushing contact—our breathing, heavy under the effort, mixing in the air—our eyes meeting after the physical encounter, seeing what effect our behavior has on each other—contact—contact. Compare this with the incredible, out-rageous distance of the contained, evenly breathing analyst sitting (or resting) concealed behind his patient's supine figure . . . under the pseudo-rationalization that it helps his patient if he remains aloof, intact, separate, blank, unidentified, unfeeling, safe, dead . . . he should never show feelings—primal sin, this—he should be but a machine, computing and analyzing. God! No wonder the inter-minable length of treatment in analysis, the poor results, the wasted horrible years of agony, and the dried-up, defensive, rigid, dehuman-ized frauds called psychoanalysts.

Two years ago, Henry, a forty-nine-year-old patient who is more than six feet tall, began to reach for his customary cigarette while in my office. I asked: "Do you have to smoke now?" (I've noticed that whenever an anxious moment erupts most smokers reach for a cigarette.) He laughed and said: "No, but I want to." Which got us quickly into a discussion of *needing* to smoke versus *wanting* to smoke. (Do you know how often these two concepts are confused? It starts at day one when the parent starts giving the child what he wants, which is very often diametrically opposed to what he needs!) Henry had smoked about three and one-half packs a day and at times literally chain-smoked. He was "afraid of giving them up cold turkey" because he "might get too nervous." He, himself, laughed at this rationalization and, continuing to laugh, said he could cut down but he couldn't cut them out altogether: "They're bigger than I am." I listened to his words while gazing at his towering height and was struck with the discrepancy. Immediately I asked him to put his pack of cigarettes on the floor in an upright position and stand to his full height looking down at the pack. I then asked him to say, directly to the cigarettes, what he had just said about them. With a broad smile he looked down, his shoulders bowed, and repeated the words in a meek, placating tone: "You're bigger than I am." I asked him to repeat this again, addressing the cigarettes this time. "Cigarettes, you're bigger than I am . . . no (pulling himself up taller and straightening his shoulders) . . . *I'm* bigger than you are." I asked: "Who's bigger?" He answered strongly: "*I* am, *I'm* bigger." I then said: "Tell it to them," pointing to the pack of cigarettes still on the floor. He looked down, throwing his chest out, and said loudly: "I'm bigger than you are."

We then sat face to face and discussed the problem. I told him I gave up smoking several years ago when I realized how demoralized I felt to be controlled by a stinking little weed. The heights, or rather degraded depths, of my demoralization was reached when, suddenly discovering myself without cigarettes while on a hike at a campgrounds in a New York State park and with no stores around, I became desperate for a cigarette and picked up some butts . . . little ones, at that . . . from the ground and did them in.

Back to my patient: to further help him "overcome" I told him that with each cigarette he reached for he had only to say: "Here and Now I don't *have* to smoke this cigarette." We discussed the fact that he *wants* to and that this is different from his *having* to. When he left the office he was resolved to cut down on his smoking and equally resolved not to cut it out altogether.

One week later he arrived with a list of days since the last session and numbers indicating a range of nine to seventeen cigarettes with an average of thirteen per day. One immediate result of his decreased intake was his ability to breathe more deeply. "It feels good to breathe for a change." Also he felt stronger about himself. We went through the size difference again and he started out defending his taking just ten cigarettes a day: a little poison instead of a lot on the grounds that they made him *feel good!*

Lobotomy would make you feel even better—no pain at all. *But feeling better is not the goal of therapy . . . feeling comfortable is not the goal of therapy . . .* these may very well, from time to time, be by-products. The real goal is getting yourself together as a person, experiencing and overcoming . . . meeting each challenge . . . experiencing and relating honestly to other persons . . . discovering your potential for constant growth . . . exploring whatever creative potential you can find within yourself . . . exploring . . . feeling . . . discovering.

Well . . . I want to tell you of a personal result of that session with this patient: I inaugurated a new rule—no smoking in my office! I am now amazed that I ever condoned smoking in my office—how inconsistent can one be! And with this new ruling a deluge of complaints from my smoking patients was hurled at me, and I was challenged severely for this autocratic rule and I had to work diligently getting my thinking and feeling caps together in order to come up with the following three reasons, which I presented to my challengers:

(1) I work with anxiety—it's the motive force—the mobilizing energy—nature's alarm to wake up, change something, and live. Cigarettes, like all other addictions, allay anxiety and lull us to sleep and therefore interfere with my patients' work with me and mine with them.

(2) Nicotine's a poison. If I permit smoking right there in front of me I thereby passively condone it. I use my prescription pad for all kinds of things, but I never use it for tranquilizers or other drugs . . . all toxic enough to necessitate extra work on the liver's part to detoxify the chemicals, to say nothing of the harmful side effects. Since, in my work with patients, I prescribe no drugs, why should I passively condone (by not actively condemning) nicotine use?

(3) Why should I have to inhale all the damn cigarette smoke! (Cigarette smoke is potent enough that inhalation in a room where a cigarette has been smoked can cause doubling of the fetal heart rate in a pregnant woman exposed to the smoke.) I refuse to have

my lungs poisoned—besides I have to live in it, my office being my living room, and I smell the cigarette smoke for hours after my last patient has left.

I must say, the more addicted smokers gave me the roughest time in the form of vigorous arguments, but ultimately they all respected my rule. Even a young woman who is a heavy smoker, the ex-junkie with the flashbacks, was able to tolerate my restriction. And now that I've effected this rule, I wonder how come it took me so long to set it into motion. Afraid of taking the risk and jumping into their anger outbursts?

Another smoker, Selma, aged twenty-one, said it was time to give up cigarettes because she had a terrible lingering cough and sore throat that she couldn't get rid of. But she was afraid to give up cigarettes because she didn't want to gain back the weight she had lost on a very successful dieting regime. In the session that was planned for working on her getting rid of her cigarette habit, she played around a bit, showed that she was not committed to stopping *right away,* but rather wanted to *explore* stopping because she thought she "should" stop. When I asked her to place the pack in front of her on the floor and carry out a dialogue, the following conversation, condensed, ensued:

S: You're bad for me—you cause me harm.

E: Address the cigarettes by name.

S: Marlboro, you don't treat me right; you give me a sore throat and a sore chest.

E: Now give them a voice and have them respond.

S: We don't cause anything . . . we're just inanimate . . . you do what you want with us.

E: Now respond to that.

S: Well, you make me feel so good. I want you.

E: Now be the cigarettes.

S: We're just inanimate—it's up to you—you can do anything with us.

E: Now be your lungs talking to you.

S: Oh, no! (Laughs) We hurt—we're all sore. Why do you

204

poison us? (To me:) Gee! I guess that's what I'm really doing to myself and what I've done with overeating too—poisoning myself. (Becomes teary-eyed)

E: Respond to your lungs.

S: You're right, I hurt myself when I hurt you. I can't even breathe right.

E: Now talk to the cigarettes.

S: (Angered and determined) Marlboro, that's the end of you. I won't poison myself with you anymore! (Whereupon she got up, picked up the pack of cigarettes, and hurled them into the wastebasket.) She ended the session feeling strong, good about herself, liking herself more, and with an emergence of greater confidence in herself. To my knowledge she has not resumed smoking.

One of the important steps in therapy is the reestablishment of contact with the body, parts of which are often blocked off from feeling and disinherited and disowned. Common body parts for women to disown are the breasts. Complaints vary from "they're too big and sloppy; they embarrass me" to "they're too small; they're just little buttons; I'm flat-chested; I don't look like a woman." I've encountered complaints about undersize more commonly than oversize.

I saw a beautiful young woman in her upper twenties who is a talented dancer. In talking about feelings of longing for having children and describing the feelings within her body, she said that when she thought of a newborn she didn't think of nursing and she said she didn't like her breasts: "They are out of balance with the rest of me." She is a slim woman of slight build and actually her small breasts are in perfect proportion with the rest of her body. So she was somheow separating her breasts from the rest of her body, and while she had fantastic contact with and awareness of most of the rest of her body . . . her movements looking much like a dance . . . her breasts were isolated and she had no feeling in them. I asked her to touch her breasts and she began to poke her fingers in them, saying she didn't like them, they were too small, they had no feeling. I asked her to become aware of her hands and she suddenly saw that her palms were far away from her breasts . . . that she was keeping her palms from touching her breasts and that her fingertips alone were poking into her breast tissue. As soon as she became aware of this, she put her full palms in contact with her breasts, cupping her hands over her breasts. Her face, which had looked strained and hard, almost contemptuous, suddenly softened; her face took on a look of surprise as she exclaimed: "They feel warm! . . . and I feel warm . . . and they just fit . . . they *are* in balance with the rest of me . . . they feel good . . . I feel good!" . . . and her face, which had been drained of its color, took on a pink glow.

She had disowned her breasts, felt or rather unfelt them to be unsightly, disproportionate, cold, and without feeling. In owning her breasts, accepting them by really allowing herself to feel them for the first time, they "fit just right," became perfectly proportioned, warm, and gave the rest of her a good feeling.

When we disown a part of our body, we lose contact with it, literally give away the feeling in that part, and thus distort it. When we own it—regain possession—we regain contact—energy flows through the part and we feel it to be part of our synchronous whole.

My second saga on breasts starts with a forty-year-old woman patient, Patricia (I was going to say "young woman" and omit her age, which is a misleading number of years, for she has a lithe, slim body, and moves like a twenty-year-old). I had been seeing her for several months when suddenly she announced one day that she had been thinking of breast surgery to enhance the size of her small breasts and wanted first to know what I thought of the idea . . . which led us into a discussion of her breasts. She believed the rest of her body to be beautiful and beautifully proportioned and the only blemish was her "almost nonexistent breasts." We talked about her experience with her breasts and she spoke of how, as an adolescent, she had looked forward to growing breasts. Later, when the first of her two children was born she had tried to nurse her baby and, due to faulty attitudes and care on the part of the nursing staff, she developed severe sores on her nipples. By the time she got medical attention, the cracks on her nipples had become so bad she decided the pain wasn't worth it and she gave up nursing. Patricia, however, was capable of experiencing pleasurable sensations in her breasts during sexual contact.

After all this talk, I asked her to feel her breasts, which she did in somewhat the same manner as the dancer I have already described, poking her fingertips gingerly into her breast tissue. On asking her to become aware of what her fingers were doing, she laughed and said: "They're poking into me." She then became aware of how she was holding her palms away from her breasts as if to avoid contact. As soon as she became aware of this avoidance, she embraced her breasts fully with her cupped palms and described the warm sensation this gave her. She felt the warmth not only in her hands but in her breasts and then suffused throughout her body. She talked of the *feeling* in her breasts, then, for the first time rather than their *size*. However, at the end of the session she reverted to questions about surgically increasing the size with "some plastic stuff the surgeons are using." I told her we'd continue the discussion at our next session. I could not resist, however, at some point during this session when she was in touch with how "good my breasts feel," slipping in the remark that plastic has no *feeling*.

The following week she announced, with a smile, that she had thought it over and that she *liked* the *feel* of her breasts, that they felt proportionate to the rest of her body, and that she didn't need or want a breast operation.

How many contactless women go from one doctor to another, from one surgeon to another, fixing this part and that part, medicating this ache and that ache, when all they really need is to *get in touch with themselves!* Oh, you doctors, stop taking advantage of these women's misery! Don't succumb to their desperate longing for surgical or medical mutilation—stop counting your teeth and count their scars instead. Help them get in touch . . . don't mutilate further their contact with themselves! Once they are separated from themselves they can never be part of any duet, can never sing together with a man, with a child—can be only a part, never a whole, nor a whole part of a wholeness. Your sedatives separate them, your knives separate them—and when they are separated out, with their tranquilized minds, their sedated passions, their perfect noses and plastically protruding breasts—who will ever put them together again?

Here again I think on the difference, the vast gulf, between need and want . . . and how these often are in opposition to one another. Patricia wanted big breasts; she needed to establish contact with the breasts already hers and which she contemptuously denied. Giving her big plastic "jugs" would not only not have given her what she *needed,* but might have prevented her from ever achieving it . . . from ever accepting the *contact with what was already hers.*

I find, over and over again, a burst of relief coming from patients when we somehow resolve the question of need versus want, when I somehow let them know that they don't *have* to get what they *want,* that they can also choose not to get what they want, especially if it is destructive and interferes with a need.

My third breast story involves a young woman gym teacher in her twenties, Kitty, who had never experienced any sensual or sexual feelings in her body for as far back as she could remember. In our second session, we talked of her masculinity and femininity—she had been involved in some sort of relationships with lesbians but denied any genital activity or sensation. She said: "I could go in the direction of men or women—I'm no place." In focusing on her feelings about her body, she said she didn't like it and again said she never had any genital sensations nor any feelings in her breasts. She disliked her breasts because "they're too small." She is five feet two inches and wears a 34A brassiere, her breasts appearing in good proportion to her body size.

E: What does "too small" mean? Small is relative.

K: No, it's not.

E: If a three-year-old girl had breasts of your size, would they be too small for her?

K: No, they'd be big.

E: Then small is relative?

K: Yes.

E: You've never had any feelings or sensations at all in your breasts?

K: No, never—they're like not there.

E: Never in your whole life?

K: No.

E: Would you feel your breasts now?

K: Yes. (She places her hands on her breasts in a firm, full-palmed grasp.)

E: How do they feel?

K: They feel firm. (Removing hands quickly)

E: Would you allow yourself to experience feeling them again?

K: Yes. (She does so.)

E: Now tell me what you experience.

K: They feel tender.

E: What does that mean?

K: Uh . . . they feel warm. (Pause)

E: And now?

K: (Broadly smiling with a glow on her face—prior to this breast episode she was feeling "dead" and "depressed.") I feel warm —the breasts feel good.

E: Whose breasts?

K: My breasts.

K: Would you repeat what you just said and own your breasts?

K: *My* breasts feel good.

E: Would you say that again?

K: (Looking quite happy by now) My breasts feel good.

E: Would you look at yourself touching your breasts and repeat that?

K: (Looking down at her hands on her breasts, continuing to smile) My breasts feel good.

By the end of this session I believe this masculine young gym teacher had begun to own back part of her rejected femininity—for the first time in her life she allowed herself to enjoy the feel of her breasts and allowed her breasts to feel a sensation of pleasurable warmth. When she said "they feel tender," I believe she meant she was feeling tender toward them.

— Another commonly disowned part of the body is the eyes. Eyes —the portals of the soul. The paranoid person gives his eyes, his sight, away to everyone else and then feels *them* looking at *him*. When he regains his own eyes, gets in touch with *his* looking at *them*, his fearful paranoia disappears. Here's an experience I had with a patient, just to give you an idea of what I mean:

Bert, who had had four years of psychoanalytic treatment before coming into therapy with me, still had difficulty, when in a business meeting, with feelings of inferiority, awkwardness, nervousness, and fears that the other men would see how dumb and incompetent he really was. He described the scene at the business meetings very vividly. He would feel that all eyes were upon him and he would keep his own eyes glued down to the papers in front of him. He felt everyone's eyes burning into him, scrutinizing him. (Recall T. S. Eliot's Prufrock who feels "fixed and formulated, wriggling on a pin.") What this patient had done was to disown his own eyes, putting them in everyone else's head . . . and he remained looking at himself. In our session together, we went through an imaginary business meeting during which I kept encouraging him to keep his own eyes in his own head and *use them*. In the fantasy he created, based on real experiences, he was able to look around and describe everyone at the meeting, what they were wearing, what they were doing. Having successfully accomplished this in fantasy in my office (the thought being father of the deed), he later, at the next business meeting, was able to accomplish the same feat in reality. He was amazed to see some people of whom he had previously been in awesome fear and whom he had thought of as being greatly self-possessed show signs of nervousness . . . others showed signs of boredom. He felt strong and self-assured, and throughout the meeting he conducted himself with remarkable competence. For the first time at these meetings he *kept his eyes in his own head and used them*, staying together with himself, and thus acted out of his intact strength.

210

At a subsequent meeting where there were bank presidents and administrators and a very powerful multimillionairess who had everyone quaking before her (she was supposed to have had her husband bumped off and have gotten away with it), Bert was able to stand up to her, resist her attempt to dominate and control the meeting, and oppose some ludicrous demands she was placing upon the group. He won the silent admiration of the "important and dignified and powerful" men who were sitting there and shaking before this dominating, aggressive woman. Bert had owned back his eyes, regained his vision, established contact with his guts, and assumed power. In an aura of glory he had stood before this indomitable woman and the entire august assemblage of bank presidents and declared in great dignity: "Mrs. Grand, I don't want to do business with you"—turned on his heel and left the meeting, with his partner following behind him. Far from losing business contacts from the men at the meeting, a past and incessant fear of his, he achieved their openly expressed admiration. And it all started with his owning back his eyes . . . using them.

Do you want to get yourself together . . . keep yourself together? *Then own your own parts* . . . accept them . . . they're yours . . . touch them . . . look at them . . . use them . . . take responsibility for them . . . they *are* your responsibility . . . they are yours . . . *they are you!*

It's not easy? It's hard work? I'll have to answer you as I do my patients when they complain to me that something I've asked them to do is hard. *Yes!* I affirm, living, too, is hard; the easiest thing for us to do is to lie in a coffin. So, once and for all, I'm not talking about *easy* . . . I'm talking about *hard* . . . *hard is good* . . . dying is easy . . . *hard is good* . . . any penis will tell you that! . . . stay with your body, it's a great teacher . . . *good therapy is hard*—simple and hard-hitting . . . *hard is good* . . . *is real* . . . *is life* . . . *is nature.*

Thou and I; the end of therapy, the beginning of life.

10

HOW TO AVOID BECOMING A VEGETABLE: DOUBT, DISSENT, AND ANGER OR THE OUNCE OF PREVENTION

How to escape the engulfment by the vegetative process . . . the vegetable with its passivity, immobility, its immersion in acceptance? How to release my human being in a healthy marriage between my animal and my spiritual selves?

My questioning hooks me into my animality; my doubts spur my reaching beyond my grasp; the force of my anger impresses my energy on my environment and creates change.

Questioning . . . dissent. My very emergence into psychiatry was born out of my dissensions. To go back for a moment, I graduated from Olney High School in Philadelphia at the age of sixteen, having been the first freshman in the history of that school to get a part in a senior play—Puck in *A Midsummer Night's Dream* with my mischievous pigtails swinging as I leaped upon the props of boulders and logs. This historical fact raised the possibility that I was cut out for an acting career, and a scholarship I then received to a dramatic school (Rel Mar Players) convinced me utterly. So, my high-school diploma still fresh, I said to my mother: "I'd like to go to New York to get on the stage," and my mother replied: "Yes, if that's what you want to do . . . I trust you to take care of yourself," and my father concurred on both counts. Maybe the incessant Elizabethan poems and Shakespearean monologues emerging in loud tones from my room convinced them, too, that I had talent. They later told me that they felt the only way I could get it out of my system was for them to let me go. So go I did, and for three years I knocked around New York, making the usual round of dramatic agencies, casting calls, getting small parts in nonpaying theatre groups, supporting myself with waitress jobs and salesgirl jobs at Macy's. And then I finally decided that I was too dumb about things and that maybe if I went to college I'd get smarter, so after three years I entered the college establishment still thinking that I might thus find a means to better support myself while I continued to pursue my acting career.

It was in my junior year at college (University of Pennsylvania) that the first major revolution in my life took place. It started with a book that a friend gave me and insisted I read. I was overwhelmed by the book . . . suddenly saw myself, my family, my world in a new and startling light . . . my intense puritanical naïveté (which had survived those three years of hobnobbing with theatre people) was being shattered by words. And how I rebelled against those words. I argued with every page, every paragraph . . . took copious notes, arguing my own points of view at laborious length; for every page read, I wrote two or three argumentative ones of my own. Had the author been alive, I'm sure I would have contacted him and belabored him in person. My questionings enlivened the book's contents for me . . . and enlivened also myself.

My life and its direction immediately changed . . . I came home from the university one day and quietly announced to my mother: "I would like to go to medical school." And just as quietly she said: "Yes, if that's what you want to do," complying as readily as she had to my acting plans six years previously. I then immediately changed my major to premed, got a scholarship, and was on my way.

214

That book, which caused my personal internal and external revolution, was Freud's *Basic Writings*. I valued his brilliant discoveries, but my questioning of him, my anger at his negativity and his Victorian-male chauvinism provoked my devotion to the subject matter of the human dilemma in general and my personal plight in particular. And through my questioning of his facts and theories, I grew . . . and grew. I was later to question him further when I discovered Harry Stack Sullivan, Karen Horney, Erich Fromm, and above all Wilhelm Reich . . . and still question more after later encountering Fritz Perls and Virginia Satir and Price Cobbs in personal workshops . . . all of whom moved me still further from the still couch . . . the still word . . . the stilled emotion. Had I not been angered at some of what Freud said, had I not doubted and questioned his points of view, had I accepted everything on faith as have so many rigid Freudians, both I and my subsequent patients would have been incarcerated on that still couch forever.

So—question me, demand, doubt, suspect, prove, disprove, argue, wonder, question . . . argue . . . doubt . . . dissent . . . and I will do likewise to you. We will put our hooks of question marks into each other, accept nothing on faith but the feelings we have . . . and we will grow and create growth in each other.

As for anger . . . someday I'm going to write a thing on the constructive uses of anger . . . blow the minds of the nice-contained-controlled-intellectualized-held-in psychotherapeutic establishment.

Anger—roar—thunderbolts—waves crashing—yelling, . . . screaming . . . the price of tranquillity—no, not the price, the prerequisite—no, more—the handmaiden! Anger is the handmaiden of tranquillity . . . they go hand in hand forever.

I received an urgent call from one of the few decent doctors (a general practitioner) I've met—an honest guy with integrity, interested in his patients and not in keeping status upmanship with his fellow club members. He had a twenty-year-old patient in a hospital who had almost successfully killed himself by cutting his wrist and then jumping out of a window in an attempt to finish the

215

job . . . result: severed median nerve and several crushed verte-
brae requiring surgery, arm cast and back brace. The patient, Larry,
had seen a psychologist for one year at college and a psychiatrist for
one month prior to his suicide try (I met this psychiatrist at a meeting later and he said he had no idea Larry was depressed!). The
general practitioner had heard I had a "new type of treatment" and
hoped it would help his patient. I agreed to see Larry and suggested
his parents come too.

The trio entered my office, the father a loud, effusive, blustering
man; the mother stiff, rigid, masklike; Larry, moving with difficulty,
a brace covering his entire back and shoulders, his left arm in a cast
and numb, pale fingers protruding. In that first session everyone
looked straitjacketed, especially the mother. So . . . I started on
her . . . getting her to move around the room and act foolish . . .
and, after resisting real hard (which only made me insist harder),
she broke through . . . and for the first time in her marriage this
board of a woman acted silly . . . which broke the ice and started
some flow going. Later, when I focused on Larry, he was totally
without visible emotion . . . a sitting, braced encyclopedia . . .
full of intellectual high-sounding phrases. I told him to cut the crap
. . . accused him of copping out from his feelings by using words—
this is a guy who has kept all his feelings in . . . an expert in talking "about" his feelings and never expressing or exposing them . . .
a total stranger to his parents . . . stiff as his back brace. But he
kept bullshitting with words and phrases just the same, avoiding my
eyes, and giving lectures to the air. I began to get angry, yelled at
him, told him I didn't like his copping out and his wiping me out
by not looking at me. Would he just stay with expressing his feelings?
I asked. He was startled by my anger . . . got tenser . . . but his
intellectual phrases kept pouring out. I then impatiently cut through
his crappy defenses and in exasperation told him to stop talking and
just scream. Much resistance . . . when Larry screamed, finally, it
had a profound effect on his parents—for the first time . . . for the
very first time including even the wrist cutting, window jumping,
hospital surgery, and near death of their son . . . they heard his

torment, listened to its overtones, and reacted to it. Wow—they heard that scream for days and days afterward! And . . . by the end of that first session, Larry was allowing me to hold his hands, was looking warmly into my eyes, and was genuinely smiling. By the second visit, his mother's rigid face had loosened . . . his father was softened and ready to change his provocative behavior . . . and Larry was ready to relate to me and to move in therapy toward contact with his real being.

Anger! It wasn't until I got angry at Tom, a 425-pound dying man, a brilliant creative writer . . . who, after my first therapy encounter, went back to poisoning himself with gormandizing . . . it wasn't until I really blasted him that he decided to stop the bullshitting games and commit himself to getting well. He said none of his former psychiatrists and analysts (including six months of hospital psychiatrists who were treating him for his "problem") ever got angry at him. My anger made me real to him—and him real to himself. So for the first time, after all the brilliant gamesmanship he had played with psychiatrists (and *they with him*)—games that subdued both them and him—he went on to accept his own voracious anger, which was turned inward against himself in his voracity and gormandizing. He began to look for a victim in his life instead of victimizing himself. We devised a sign for him to put on his refrigerator door reading: "Find the Victim"—a device to remind him of his true anxiety and anger whenever someone pushed him around, an anxiety that led him to eat instead of pushing back, literally *pushing in* instead of *pushing out*. He went on to accept responsibility for making himself fat and sick, to accept the challenge of changing, to accept *life* instead of death.

Anger! Beautiful—natural—real—*life's* partner along with love and joy.

When Alma, a fifty-year-old doctor of philosophy, went on an alcoholic binge, breaking an agreement we had made, and called to tell me about it in a drunken stupor, I blasted her on the phone . . . she blasted me back . . . and goddamn if she didn't cut the boozin' and come in to soberly work on her hangups. In that session following the angry telephone hassle she allowed herself to be mothered, sitting on my lap and crying, letting me comfort her. She had never allowed herself to look helpless before for fear of ridicule and rejection, and at this session, allowing herself to be cradled on my lap, she faced the negativity she had always felt toward her own mother who had been both severely rejecting and demanding.

Extra! . . . *Extra!* . . . read all about it . . . come get your "new type of treatment"—a human being . . . being real . . . brand new idea! . . . be real with patients . . . express real feelings . . . *Extra!* . . . *Extra!*

Again, those goddamn books on psychology and "how to do it" for parents that tell you how to piss away your anger in closeted verbal gamesmanship called "understanding your child"—crap! The anger doesn't get pissed away—it backs up and forms an obstruction to all the other feelings—so you come off sounding *nicely icy*—Yich!

A good yell is worth a thousand words and saves a dozen years on the couch—and even saves your life! YAY-Y-Y-Y-Y-Y-Y-Y-y-y-y-y-y-y-y-y-y-y-y-y—!!!!

One of the best ways to keep ourselves rooted in a vegetable garden is to fertilize ourselves with the myth of the superiority of authority figures. On the other hand, when we start seeing our parents and all other authorities (teachers, preachers, judges, doctors, presidents) as *persons* who love, hate, fuck, shit, swallow myths, wallow in pettinesses and self-interest, have neurotic hangups, prejudices, idiosyncrasies, we are already well on the road to allowing our own animal persons to grow and develop—moving our open eyes to look at the scene that *is,* tuning in to the movements, behaviors, actions, deeds—all the animal acts of the human animals around us. (The fraudulent hypocrisy of our succession of presidents talking peace and acting war is one of the biggest vegetabilization processes our nation has had imposed on it! Thanks, Daniel Ellsberg, for making this so clear to us—you're beautiful.)

From the beginning there have been some animal types—men in

Congress—men and women in the vociferous, moving minority-now-become-majority who refused to vegetabilize themselves out of their alive animal awareness: they are growing and spreading . . . their doubts, dissents and angers are growing. *Animality, like vegetability, is contagious*—it's catching on—if the freaks and dropouts could learn to respect and care for the beauty of their intact animal bodies and brains instead of poisoning these with vegetabilizing drugs, if the authority figures (starting with parents) became people themselves exposing their human vulnerabilities, if so-called pigs became persons with one another, the humanizing revolution in America would truly succeed. How do you avoid becoming a vegetable? Be an animal . . . a human one . . . see that others are, also . . . use your eyes, your ears, your smell, your touch, your taste, your brain, your heart, your belly, your body . . . use, use, move, use—be, move, use.

I may not survive my obeisance to authorities—I *will* survive my questioning of them. The problem is—will they? And what will become of you and your fraternal order, O Caduceus Wearer, when we laymen start to question, when we women start to refuse your lucrative whipping out of our wombs . . . when we find other doctors worthy of the name who respect our flesh?

You need our help . . . we laymen will help you humanize yourselves by our doubts and questionings of you . . . by our revealing our angers against you and allowing ourselves to see your angers, your frailties, your errors, your humanity.

And now—I want to reach out to you out there. Right now, are you feeling uptight, hemmed in, pressured? Give a *loud yell* . . . when was the last time in your life you yelled? . . . crack your cheeks, open your mouth, bulge your eyes out to the limit and YELLLLLLLL! Get *it* (whatever the *it* is in your particular case) *out*—when you empty *it* out you'll feel relaxed . . . and energized . . . and ready. If you're surrounded by uptight neighbors with thin walls, get a big pillow and do your yelling into it—or go into the woods—or close the windows of your car—and let loose. Remember—get so you can remember what it was like to yell with

219

your whole body. At one time very early in your life before the culture started clamping down on you, you knew what it was to yell with all your tissues . . . get to that state again—get up a full body yell, not just with your throat—and feel that energy flow! And you speed freaks, a trip on speed just doesn't compare with the rush of a full body yell—try it.

Look—stop the book—my words can't give you as much as what you can give yourself with some good, full body yells. Get the pillow if you need one—and *let go!* And while you're at it, do some arm and leg or fist and feet poundings if you feel like it. If your yells get you in touch with some feelings—like sadness with tears or anger with greater yells or fear with shrieks—let them happen, too. Let it all out and let the energy flow . . . let those electrical currents charge through your tissues—this kind of electricity is magnificent —this kind of trip is *toward contact*—stay with it, let it all happen, let your body sing to its animal rhythm. Even a little yell, even a bare ounce worth, goes an awfully long way.

And look, I don't think you have to be afraid of letting loose; chances are, if you've gotten this far in reading this book, you have a built-in mechanism that will limit you to stay within the bounds your organism can tolerate. If, however, you feel yourself too uptight to follow my suggestion right now, if you feel something might break if you let too much yelling out, trust that feeling, trust that uptight feeling, use your own judgment and reject my invitation for a yell. It's OK for you to resist right now . . . maybe tomorrow you'll feel like chancing it, like being adventurous, exploratory, experimental.

I'm paying so much attention to yelling because mostly I meet people with the stifled shout, the hunched shoulders, the held-in breath. If, on the other hand, you are one of those uncontrollable yellers, screaming out at any provocation, you have to go the other way on your trip: sit still and quietly contemplate your navel, its excursions, the pulsations of your breathing—feel the energy coming in with the air that enters your nostrils, windpipe, and lungs, ballooning out your abdomen with the diaphragmatic relaxations.

If you're a screamer, things are going out of you all the time and you're not allowing anything to come in—spend some time letting things *come in*—let your breath come in; keep your mouth shut and let others' words come in; look with your eyes and let the others' eyes come in—this trip will take you toward greater contact than is possible in any of your yells. Listen to silence instead of the sound of your own probably blaming, accusatory voice. If you listen intently enough, you'll hear your body singing to its animal rhythm, which your yells have been blotting out.

I guess there's no single simple formula that is good for all of us except for breathing—full, expansive, cleansing animal breathing. Do it now—but not the upside-down way you've been taught in your militaristic-type gym classes: "Pull your belly in, push out your chest"—all wrong! (No wonder there's so much damn emphysema!) Watch an infant or a dog breathe and relearn what once you knew. *What a sad state that we even have to learn something so basic as breathing.* Breath is the staff of life—let's breathe correctly. Imagine a balloon in your belly attached to a straw that comes up and out of your mouth. Suck in the air as if inhaling through that straw and imagine the balloon in your belly filling with air. Keep your chest relaxed and it won't push out. Watch your belly balloon out during inhalation—watch it go in with exhalation . . . do it several times . . . if you get light-headed, OK—let it happen. If your body starts to tingle, to vibrate, OK—let it express the energy flow and movement in whatever way happens. Let your body and your breathing happen.

One problem with the average policeman or soldier is that he sees himself as representing a larger body, while giving up his selfhood to follow the dictates of this larger group. We all share in this giving up of our individuality whenever we renounce our personal responsibility for our actions and blame things on our parents, our organization, our culture, human nature. Some people go to the extreme of almost always using, for the personal pronoun, the collective or editorial "we" (or "you"), which is a subtle way of shirking personal responsibility for their statements and actions.

221

"Well, when *we* get *our* office moved *we'll* start paying more attention to *the* wife and less to *the* practice," said a middle-aged lawyer whose wife was complaining he wasn't paying enough attention to her. *"You* know, when *you* work hard all day dealing with troubled clients *you* can't spend time with *your* wife at the end of the day—*you're* just too tired out." He sat stiffly in his bulging flesh offering me the foregoing statements in an uninvolved, lecturing tone as though pleading someone else's case. When I interrupted his lecture and asked him to repeat it, converting all the "our's" and "you's" to "I's' " he dropped his lecturing tone, his face flushed, he began to let some feelings pour into his words, and he looked more alive.

I . . . say it: I, I, I, I, I, I, I. Say it some more—start with "I"—it's a great place to start! I-I-I-I-I-I. Now go on with: I am, I am, I am, I am, I am, I am. And now finish with the ungrammatical but real: I am me, I am me, I am me. And now go over to the mirror and repeat the entire litany, looking at your face, your eyes, your mouth, your chin as you say the words, letting your face come into your eyes. And remember, you began life with the I. When you renounce the I, you renounce life. I'm not talking of pathology here, I want to stay with the preventive steps you and I can take to stay alive . . . so I'll stop talking of renouncing. I want to *affirm* myself, I want you to affirm yourself. There is a you transcending the roles you play, an I transcending my role—this you, this I, needs affirmation. Come, join me in this affirmation. Say with me: I like me, I like me, I like me, I like me, I like me. And when you can look at yourself saying this (literally, get a mirror and try it—don't be like Galileo's calumniators who refused to look at truth through his telescope), when you can find the place in yourself where this statement is true (and it is true somewhere beneath whatever layers of self-contempt you heap over it . . . or you wouldn't be alive right now), when you've succeeded in finding that place in you where "I like me" applies, then go on to say: I love me, I love me, I love me, I love me, I love me. I see some of you resisting, I see your tears of denial, I hear your complainings of "but

I don't—I don't love me—there's nothing to love" . . . and I insist, say it anyway—say it—keep saying it—feed yourself—dammit, nourish yourself, just say it as if you mean it—listen to yourself saying it, watch yourself saying it, close your eyes and feel yourself saying it. Give yourself a healthy shot of this every day—sing it, celebrate it, hear the glory in the I. And once you have this feeling of I, you can feel the I in others beneath their layers of defense and self-contempt . . . and you can allow the "others" to be like you and also different from you.

No one else can give you the I feeling; no matter how greedily you clutch at others for this, no matter how many security marriages you enter, herein you must feed yourself. The conflict between you and your culture requires a balance: society demanding your I be diminished to conform to the social group, you affirming the aggrandizement of the I—back and forth, back and forth. The whole damn culture would collapse altogether if society's demands alone were met, for how can a society of vegetables produce animals who move not only themselves but who move the whole culture along.

Now, once you have felt the surge through your body that comes from releasing, letting go, the phony humilities and other excuses and from getting in touch with the nourishing flow in the words of self-love and affirmation of self, you can then go to the other necessary route to alive awareness, but I wouldn't suggest you take this step until you really feel the glory in the I. When you are ready, look at yourself and say: I don't like me. Immediately these words, if you are listening, may release a store of things about yourself that are not self-affirming, either things from your past that people heaped on you, or physical or personality attributes you disapprove of in yourself, and so forth. With enough self-affirmative grounding, you can let these negative things emerge and face them as squarely as their positive counterpart—by facing them instead of denying them you might even find the strength to change them or at least to learn to live with them.

And breathe while you're doing all this—never give that up—

223

focus on your breathing above all else. Feel how good it is to be simply an animal breathing fully.

And now I feel as though I'm approaching the end—there are pieces still floating around, not tied neatly together—the drama is still unfolding—and I will leave the loose ends flowing for you to tie together in your own way. I am eager, above all else, to bring this to you now—before any one of you has one needless hysterectomy, or mastectomy, or prostatectomy . . . before you desist from asking the one question that may save your life . . . before you go under life with one more drug or one more night's television coffining . . . before you give your guts away and vegetabilize yourself for good.

Come . . . now with me . . . contact those guts . . . let your focus bring them together sharper . . . feel the tension . . . the anxiety . . . the *discovery* of your innards . . . let the flow emerge through your total person and out into all that you now, here and now, become aware of.

Do not resist . . . resist; hold back . . . do not hold back; hold your breath . . . breathe.

Stay with and reach beyond all your contradictions, your "visions and revisions that a minute will reverse" . . . accept your faiths . . . your disbeliefs; your angers . . . your placatings; your acceptings . . . your dissentings; your hatings . . . your lovings. Accept all your idiocies—and your brilliances . . . your greatnesses—and your insignificances . . . your crazinesses—your saneness . . . your guts . . . your head . . . your body . . . your vagina . . . your penis . . . your breasts . . . your testes . . . accept—reject—accept—*For you and I are all of these—we are human.*

224